W9-BKJ-379

*f*P

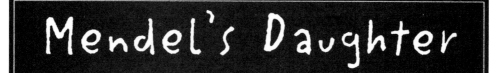

Mendel's Daughter

Gusta Lemelman · Martin Lemelman

Free Press

New York London Toronto Sydney

FREE PRESS

A Division of Simon & Schuster, Inc.
1230 Avenue of the Americas
New York, NY 10020

FREE PRESS and colophon are
trademarks of Simon & Schuster, Inc.

For information about special discounts for bulk purchases,
please contact Simon & Schuster Special Sales:
1-800-456-6798 or business@simonandschuster.com

Designed by Jaime Putorti

Manufactured in the United States of America

10 9 8 7 6 5 4 3 2 1

Library of Congress Cataloging-in-Publication Data is available

ISBN-13: 978-0-7432-9162-0
ISBN-10: 0-7432-9162-X

In loving memory of my mother Gusta,
my Aunt Yetala, my Uncle Simon, my Aunt Regina,
my Aunt Jenny, her husband Feivel, their son Eli,
my grandmother Malkah,
and my grandfather Menachem Mendel.

May their memory be a blessing.

For my Uncle Isak — until one hundred and twenty.

To my dear brother and sister-in-law, Bernard and Diane.

And, of course, to Monica — my partner through life.

Der Mentsch tracht, un Gutt lacht.
Man plans, and God laughs.

Yiddish saying

Mendel's Daughter

"I've always felt that
MY MOTHER
lived in a world of magic.

She always claimed
that her FATHER,
MENACHEM MENDEL,
spoke to her in dreams.

And then there was
my AUNT YETALA...

Until the day she died,
she spoke of
an ANGEL of GOD
who saved her from the Nazis.

Needless to say, I was skeptical."

MY MOTHER died on December 8, 1996.

last

night,

SHE spoke to me.

"Oy,
mein tayereh
Mattaleh,
my precious
Martin,"
she said,
"you now have
52 years."

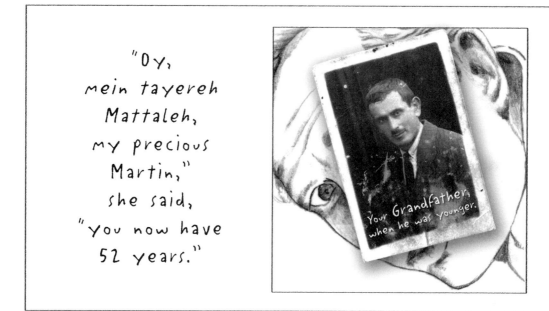

Your Grandfather, when he was younger.

"This is the same age from my FATHER,
when he was murdered."

"Listen to me,
Mattaleh!

Sometimes
your MEMORIES
are not your
OWN."

PART ONE: GERMAKIVKA
1919-1939

My Nephew, Eli, photographed June 15, 1938.
My sister Jenny's only child.

OUR family lived in the town of GERMAKIVKA.
Now is in Ukraine, before was in the Soviet Union.
When we live there it was POLAND.

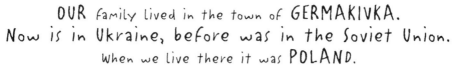

ГЕРМАКІВКА

I could look out on the main
street. It was beautiful outside
the house.

Out in the street was trees and ground
and houses and horses and cows and dogs.
Everything.
The front was the main street. By the
corner was a big cross about eight foot.

The house where we live has one floor and a tin roof.
There was four rooms. In the back, a distance of about three miles,
was the woods of Maravinitz.

The Christians in the town, they like the FATHER. They like the MOTHER, too.

I think this saved us later.

We have the only well in the street. Even Isia, my youngest brother, remembers when the FATHER has it built. It was a good new well.

Before, everybody on the street went someplace else for the water.

After, all the houses came to us for water.

Everyone, always, was welcome in our house.

I remember birds used to come sit down near our front door.

When you come in the house, was a little hallway. This is how we get into the house. There is a wooden ladder going up to the attic. Nothing is in the attic.

To the right was a door to the bedroom and straight was a door into the kitchen.

I was sleeping all the time
with my sister Jenny
before she gets married.
The two younger sisters
was sleeping together
in another bed.
There was four in the room.

The mattresses were filled
with straw.

The blanket was made of feathers, and in the winter
it was cold like a piece of ice.

We would run to the kitchen
and get dressed.
We was taking turns sleeping
on the oven in winter.
It was very warm over there.
Everybody has a blanket
with a lot of feathers made
from the ducks and geese,
not from chickens.
This makes the hard oven
soft.

Every day, from when I was little, until I was big,
we all woke up at 8 o'clock, seven thirty, like this. We have
grishig, a cooked cereal, bread and butter and milk for breakfast.
Sometime we have a *Flampletzle*. I tell you about this later.

The MOTHER has a lot of kids to cook for. We are seven children.

My sister Jenny  was 18 months older than me.

Then came me. Then came Yetala. Two years younger.

Then Regina. She is younger than Yetala by a year and a half.

Then comes the brother, Isia, the youngest.

Simon was the older. He is our half-brother.

Our other half-brother Chunah

gets married and leaves for Argentina in 1933.

We have a big garden and in our garden walnuts was growing, cherries was growing. No apples, but pears and the red big plums. We have potatoes and string beans. Our garden was all the way until the railroad tracks. Until the tracks was ours and after the tracks was our fields, too. Our fields go right to the train station. The next station to Germakivka was a town by the name of Ivana Pusta. This was the last stop for the train. That was the stop, later, that they put the Jews in the cars and take them away.

We have flowers,
a lot of flowers
in our garden, too.
Roses, lilacs.
You know,
it was special to look
when the roses was blooming.
Then when they die,
we have the rose heads.
You call them rosehips.

14

We used to cut the yellow pieces from the rosehips with the scissors because this was the bitter part.

Then my Mother used to mash the rest with sugar, and let it sit overnight. Then the preserve juice, she would cook.

It was like a liquor, a tea.

The tea was like a tea color and it was delicious.

This was good for a sick person.

The Mother would also make the *povedal.*
Here you call prune butter.
This was my mother's special job.
By us we would make it and we have for the whole year.

We used to hire maybe 20 shiksas to help us to do the work, to pick the two hundred pounds plums.

I remember now. There were three sisters.

They were poor, but very nice girls.
One was intelligent. Their name was
Sadarozny. They help us in the fields
and taking the pits from the plums.

Their Father,
he gave us food in the WAR.

We would make a fire in a hole and cook the plums in a big kettle.
We would cook the plums outside in a kettle the whole night.
Cooking, mixing.
Everyone would take turns mixing, so the others should rest.
Everyone likes to eat this. The Jews. The Christians.

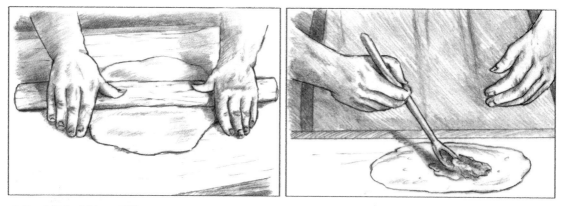

OH, MY MOTHER was never sleeping Thursday night.
She was baking and cooking and preparing for Shabbos.
Thursday night MY mother baked challah.
She bakes everything, bread, cake, cookies.
A honey cake, or a sponge cake.

She also used to make a Fluden for Shabbos.
WHAT'S A FLUDEN, you ask? A Fluden, was like here
you make a fruitcake. OH, THIS WAS DELICIOUS,
DELICIOUS! A small piece you get, not more.

WHY?

Because it was very rich. It has a lot of
fruit, eggs and nuts, raisins, walnuts.
She also puts sometimes preserves made from
pears or cherries. On the top was sprinkled
with sugar. She makes this in a long pan
and cut the pieces in squares.
Then you just pull out and eat.

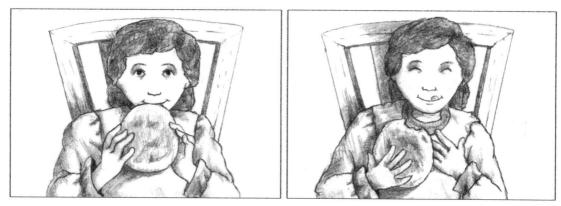

She also makes FLAMPLETZLE for the children.
That means, like here pizza. This dough was so delicious.
On the top was with butter. This was for breakfast. It was very delicious.
You put cream on it. It was flat. She would make a small one for every child.
Sometimes two would share one Flampletzle.

Everybody in the family has to do something. The children have to help with the cleaning, with the cooking, to feed the animals, like this.

When I was six years old I was making noodles. I was doing the noodles round and thin. They was so beautiful. My mother used to show the peoples.

We would eat them with chicken soup.

My MOTHER used to say that, in my life, I would work hard because I know everything.

18

The MOTHER makes the house beautiful. When she married she makes a picture of a horse with flowers, a poppy picture, a house with trees and water around.

I love the picture she make of a peacock with flowers.

She teach me to sew and to do needlework.

One time when I am working in the house, I see a
Gentile neighbor's daughter riding her bike.

I am thinking, maybe,
this girl will let me ride her bike.

But, before this happens...

This would be very nice!

"I don't want you even to go near a bike," she says.
"What are you?
An *usgelosenor*, a loose girl!
To ride the bike is not *balabatish*, proper.
YOU ARE NOT SUKOLSKY'S *SHIKSA!*"
(our Gentile neighbor's daughter).

My Mother is strict, but not like my friend Etel's *babshu*, her grandmother.
HER *BABSHU* IS WORSE.
When she is catching Etel driving the bike,
her *babshu* grabs her by the hair and pulls her off.

"A boy needs to ride a bike,"
she says. "A girl don't need to."

21

One time when she was
having words with
the **Shochet** (ritual slaughterer)
in our town, she was
sending me with the chickens
to another town.
I tell you something, she don't care
if I am hurt or healthy or having
a problem in having children one day.

I was not ten years old,
not more. She gives me three
chickens in a basket,
at least fifteen pounds.
THE BASKET WAS BIGGER THAN ME
AND SHE DON'T HAVE
NO RACHMUNIS, PITY.

So I was walking to the town of
Kriftche. I was so tired on the way
that I was sitting on the road and I
was crying. I am afraid for somebody
to give me a lift, so I don't look
for a wagon to give me a ride.

Kriftche was not so big as Germakivka, but over there was the funerals for the Jews who lived around the area. Kriftche was my father's town, but we have no relatives left there. My Grandma, and the Uncle, in the end, moved away from their house.

THEY WENT TO AMERICA.

So I take the chickens to the shochet and he kills them.

I bring them back home for the Friday night meal.

When I am thinking about Kriftche and the chickens,
I am reminding myself of something else.

Did you know my Father was three times in America?
When he was single, he was in America, and when he was with his
First wife. He goes there to make money. From New York he
travels to Pittsburgh where his relatives have a fur business.

My Father could live in AMERICA but
my Mother don't want to.
With girls she don't want to go.
WHY?
Because she conducts herself religious and
she wants her girls to be religious.
She says,
"You know, in America,
even the stones
are Treyf, unclean."

If only we go to America.

My father knows how to work with the fur, and this is what he done in America.

He also was a wonderful tailor.
When he was making a coat, was so beautiful, no question.

He makes coats for all the girls, like this one for Regincha.

This is my sister, REGINA.

MY FATHER has two favorites from his children. Isia was one because he was the youngest and a boy, and then there was my younger sister, Regina.
They all call her Regincha.
They call me Gustalah.
Regina was very smart.
She had a head.
I was older than her by four years.

I remember one time he picks up Regincha and he plays with her.

He says to her, "My little Regincha, the Mother and I will live by you in our old age."

When the Mother hears this, she says, "Zol ich nisht darleben. I should not live long enough for this to happen."

OY, MY MOTHER, SHE GETS HER WISH!

The Mother and Father was strict.

Always I have to wear my older sister's dresses. I was saying one time, "I want a new dress, too." So you know what the Mother was saying?

"You don't have to have everything!"

Even when somebody recommended a boy. My Mother asked for the information and then she said, "This one we leave for Gusta. For Jenny, better."

When Jenny finds her boyfriend, Feivel, my Father would come and give me a pinch. I should not talk to him.

These are pictures of my sister **Jenny** - from younger to older.

Everyone liked
Jenny.
She was
a happy person.

She has a lot of
friends,
**Jewish,
Christian.**

I and **Jenny** helped the **Mother**
with the cooking, the house things,
like this.

When the other children played,
we was working together.

This picture is from me and Jenny.
We was wearing the costumes
from two of her Christian friends.

Jenny married Feivel,
a nice Jewish boy.

They marry young.

Maybe a year later
she has a
baby boy, Eli.

Oy, he was such
a sweet child.

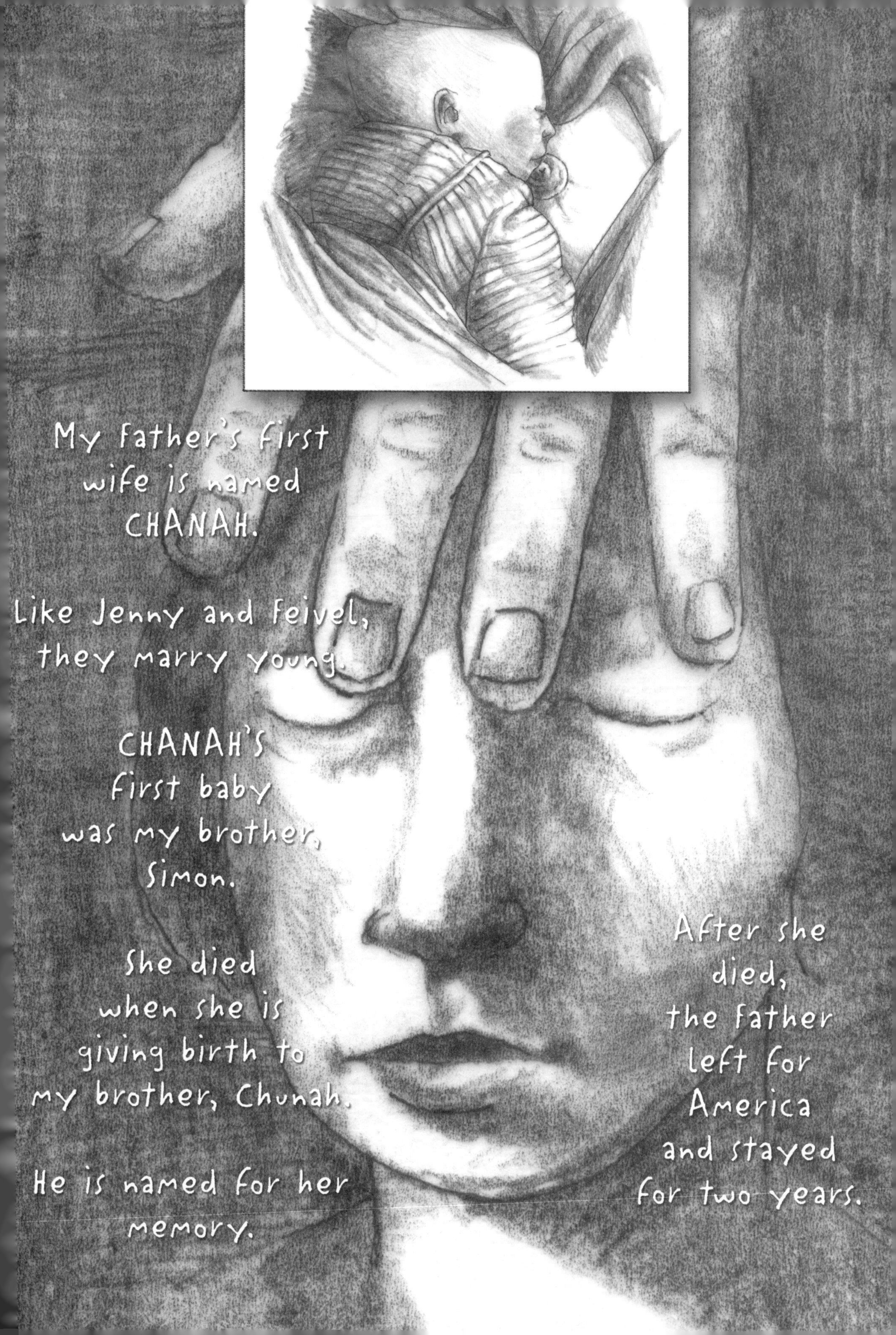

My father's first
wife is named
CHANAH.

Like Jenny and Feivel,
they marry young.

CHANAH'S
first baby
was my brother,
Simon.

She died
when she is
giving birth to
my brother, Chunah.

He is named for her
memory.

After she
died,
the father
left for
America
and stayed
for two years.

Two pictures from the **Mother** and **Father** about 1939.

My Mother, Malkah, is the sister from Chanah, the first wife of the Father. She don't want to marry.

They force her.

She is 15 years old when she marries.

They are both young.

The truth is, they learned
to love each other.

I tell you
a story,

No, a joke!

My Father
always
makes this joke
when we was
growing up.

My Father never used to buy a dress. You don't buy over there a dress.
When we was small, you don't buy a ready-made dress. My Mother used
to sew. So My Father used to buy the material and bring it home.
Oh, this was funny!
He makes believe he buys a piece of material for my sister, Jenny.
And he takes like this, so Jenny should look at the material.

BUT, you know, he really wants to buy for the MOTHER!
So he says, "No, this is not good enough for Jenny. This would only
be good for the OLTITCHKE, the old one!

OLTITCHKE, THIS IS WHAT HE IS CALLING MY MOTHER.
She was 48 years old when they kill her.

He makes this joke because he loves her. She loves him, too.
She was crying so much one time when he was sick.
She don't want to lose him.

I think they love each other very much, but,
also I think she wasn't so happy...
WHY NOT? I tell you why not.

Because the Mother was always telling us, her girls,
"Don't marry a man who already was married before."
Like she done.

I tell you something else. After the War I could marry
right when I come out from the forest. I could
marry a man, no, "a diamond." He gives me
lots of respect. But, this man had a wife
and child before the War. The Nazis was
killing his wife and child.

So I say to him, "Don't come to
see me because maybe I am afraid I
will fall in love and the Mother
don't want me to marry you."

My brothers, Simon and Chunah, call my mother "Malkah."
Because, after all, she is their Aunt but also their Stepmother.

When I was going to school, one time, I was calling my mother
"Malkah" too. When she was hearing this she was so happy.
She was thinking she is a little girl. She was 16 years old
when she got already a baby, my older sister, Jenny.
Maybe my mother is thinking she can go to school too, like me.

I never tell you we have a dog.
Everyone in our town has a watchdog.
People was breaking into the houses.
He was black and white.
We was calling him "Dog."
Oh, he was so good to me.
He would take me to school, and
I was telling him to go home.

He listens to me.

In the afternoon
I come
home from
the school and
he waits for me.
He is
such a good dog.

When Isia was maybe 4 years old, the dog bites him. Maybe he gets teased by Isia, I don't know. I don't know, but I know the **Father** has to run to the doctor to get shots for Isia because he is bitten by the dog.

What do you think the Father does?

MY FATHER is taking a stick and hitting the dog.
The FATHER is saying "NO MORE!",
and the dog is no more biting.

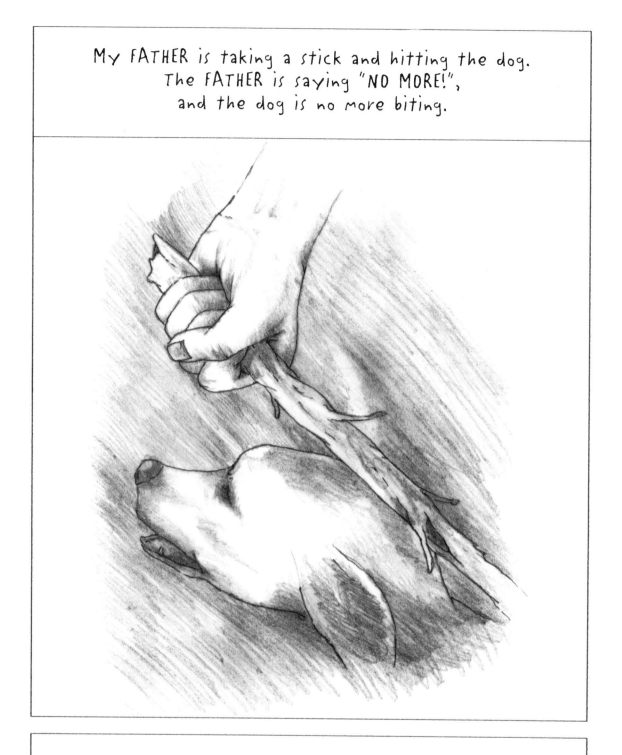

Years later my dog dies the day
the "MALACH HAMAVES," the Angel of Death
comes for the Jews of Korolivka.
He dies the day of the "Action."

I CRY FOR HIM.

The school I go to is a *Pulska Schula*, a public school. The school is a big building, one floor, many rooms. My class had, maybe, 20 children. We learn different subjects. We have reading, mathematics, Polish history, like this.

After the time when the teacher was teaching us, we have lunch.

Then was **Recess time!**
We was talking. We was reading. We was jumping rope.

We was also sitting and sewing pieces, scraps. This was a subject but we also like to do at recess. We was sitting 3-4-5 girls together and making up the *shmatkalach*, little rags.

We make beautiful.

You know in the **Pulska Schula** there was a stove to keep us warm. **One** time, **Vasil**, a Christian boy, 8 years old, takes ashes from this stove and he puts them on my bread that I have for lunch! He don't like **Jews.** I thought before this, we was friends, neighbors. He was wild when he done it.

(**When** he was older, in I think 1940, the Russians came and took him away. His sister was standing, talking to me when this happens. She is crying. I tell her they will let him out. She shouldn't cry. I go in her hallway. She collapses in her house. I run to my parents. **My mother** comes with the rosehead tea. **My father** brings water. He makes her drink. **My father,** he saw her with foam coming out of her mouth. He said, "Children, children, stay outside." **The Russians, they don't let him out.)**

Anyways, I tell the teacher about the ashes and **Vasil** gets beaten so hard, you don't have an idea.

3 o'clock I finish the **Pulska Schula.** I come home, eat, and go to **Cheder,** Hebrew School. I stay there until 5 o'clock. In my **Cheder** they teach me just **davening,** praying. They teach in **Yiddish,** not **Hebrew.** Our **Siddurim,** prayerbooks, was written in **Yiddish,** for the women.

My father, one time talk to the **Rabbi** and he says, "**Ah maydaleh,** a little girl, don't need to be so smart."

I have a good head.

The teacher gives me an "A," "good," and "needs improvement" for the grades in my report cards. You know why I get a grade "needs improvement"? I tell you. When you go to school, you should make the homework. Right? This is very important. When they give us the subject. Maybe a question about what a story means. You have to read, to know what the story is about. I don't know what the story is about. WHY? Because I don't have time to read, I was washing the dishes. I was sweeping. This makes me so mad.

I was doing the housework, helping the MOTHER. Never she was asking, "Maybe you have homework." I have homework to learn to say a poem by heart, You have to study inside first, ten times. Then you will memorize. If I have time, I would know it . But I was never having time. I was washing the dishes, instead. That was with me. If I would have somebody to push me, to make the homework, or have time for homework, I would be such a student. They don't push me.

I should have time to do this, I would be the best. But, a girl don't have to know nothing. That's what was by us.

In cheder, I have to know to daven. Nothing more. A girl was not obligated to go to shul. I go sometimes on Shabbos. A girl don't have no Bat Mitzvah. Now I see the girls. They stand with the siddur. They know when to bend, when to shake. I don't know this. In my cheder, they just teach me davening.

When a sister was born, the FATHER went to shul to name the baby. Yetala don't know to cook. Yetala don't know nothing when she grows up. WHY? Because we was doing. I and my older sister, Jenny. WHAT DID YETALA DO? She could play. She don't have the responsibility, and the younger sister, Regina, too.

Yetala

Me

Jenny

This is Jenny when she is younger. Pictures of me younger, don't survive.

I have many friends in Germakivka.
On Shabbos we went *shpatzirin*, for walks.
We have beautiful streets. People was having
respect for us. In Poland was beautiful in
the time when I grow up. Was antisemitism, too.
The friends I go walking with were Etel and
Lyncha. Everybody, together, went *shpatzirin*.
But my best friend was Etel. I have another
friend Chaya. She, they kill her. I got another
one, Nechama. They kill her. And another one,
Salya. They kill her. They kill my friends.
We was in the same school,
the same grade.

These are some of the photographs
my brother, Bernard, and I found in my
mother's nighttable after she died. They are unidentified friends.
M.L.

46

I think I told you **the father** has a store, in one room, in the house. It was like a grocery here in America. Usually everyone is going to the town markets to buy things. But, if it was a bad day, people don't go shopping in the markets. They come to us.

I work in the store from when I was 6 years old. When I come home from school, I go behind the counter and I was handling the customers.

We don't use bags in our store. No one uses bags. If someone buys a pound of potatoes or a pound of *fasolias*, beans, I make the bag from old newspapers, like this. I make a cone, like an ice cream cone and put in **the merchandise.**

We have everything you need in our store.

We was a General Store. We have two barrels. In one barrel we carry smoked fish. In another barrel we carry kerosene for the lamps. A man would bring in a jar and we fill it up. People buy one litre, two litres, five litres, like this. We have groceries. Sugar, flour, also material for the women to make clothes.

For the children was peppermints, and even **Hershey's chocolates.** I like the **Nestle's chocolates** but I think I don't eat too much because, by us, was the cakes and cookies **the Mother** bakes.

I like to work in the store.
One job I don't like is washing the glasses from the drinks we make. Now, everything comes in the paper cups. You throw away after you finish. Then we use glasses. I have to wash them in three waters. My hands get so chapped. The water is hot and the store is cold. We have no heat. One time a man gives me camphor ice to put on the fingers. This helps.

In winter and summer, all year, the **father** is riding to the markets to buy and sell schoira, merchandise. younger I come Even when I am with him. My older brother, **Simon**, helps the **father** with what we need for **the store**. One time it was a snowy day. I go with the **father** anyway.

The road to the market in **Korolivka** is rough. This is not like a road in **America**. So, when we are riding, the wagon hits a big bump and what do you know, I fall off. It takes my **father** maybe two miles before he figures out I am not on the wagon with him! He is thinking of business, buying and selling, **not me**. **No, this is not America!**

This happens on a Thursday. On Thursday he is always going to **Korolivka**. Tuesday he is always going to the market in **Milnetze**. The schoira he couldn't find in **Milnetze**, he would buy in **Korolivka**.

I love to ride to the markets in the summer.
The houses, the woods! Was beautiful.

Monday was the Yerid. This is what we are
calling the market in Germakivka. The
Father wouldn't go always, but Milnetze
and Korolivka he went every week.
I go to the yerid anytime we
need something for the house.

Sometime, let's say, a goy was
owing my father money.
The goy doesn't have the money.
So instead of money, the
goy gives my father a cow.

So then we hired a guy, I will never forget, his name was Zyitz.
He used to walk the cow to the market.
It was about 25 kilometers to Korolivka.
He used to walk the cow to Korolivka,
bring it around to the market and sell it.
That's how it was going on.
Our people making a living, many ways.

Milnetze was every Tuesday, Market days.
All the farmers was coming and bringing out whatever they had.
Chicken, eggs, milk, vegetables.
And there was also there a Gogolice, They called it.
There they brought out cows, livestock.
Like a livestock auction, a bazaar.
There was also the wholesale place over
there with the owner named Sharstein. This usually was our first stop.
It was a grocery wholesale place where we used to
buy groceries, whatever we needed.
Especially kerosene.
We used to buy because the
goyim used to buy this in our store and then sugar and
a lot of other things.
Sometimes after the business,
my father would buy me ice cream.

We was selling ice cream in our store but it was only the ready-made cones.

Here in the market was fresh, vanilla and chocolate.

Like you Mattaleh, I like vanilla. I remember, now, how funny it was when I was eating the ice cream.

Can you believe this? I used to blow on the ice cream!

The ice cream was cold and I wanted to eat it.

So I blow on it to warm it up.

Time passes and I grow older.

I was still going to the markets with the Father.

But, everything was changing. We are listening to the radio. Everybody knows the news. Everybody knows, but no one is believing.

I am thinking it will be bad for us. Very bad.

-THE SUMMER OF 1939-

I don't have no more pleasure going to the market.
Now, when the **father** says hello to his **landsleit**, his friends,
they don't talk no more from how much a chicken or a kilo of kerosene costs.

Now I am hearing about
Anschluss, Chamberlain,
the Sudetenland,
Czechoslovakia.

Now I hear the name
Hitler,
yemach shimo,
his name should be erased.

August comes and the news is the Germans and the Soviets sign an agreement. Now they are friends.

How can they be friends?

September our lives change.

Aug 23, 1939 - the Nazis and Soviets sign a Non-Agression Pact.
Sept 1, 1939 - the Nazis invade Poland.
Sept 3, 1939 - Britain, France, declare war on Germany.
Sept 14, 1939 - Rosh Hashana
Sept 17, 1939 - the Soviets invade Poland.
Sept 23, 1939 - Yom Kippur
                                        M.L.

On Rosh Hashana it is written. And on Yom Kippur it is sealed.

How many will be born and how many will pass away.

Who will live and who will die.

Who with time shortened and who with full days.

Who by fire and who by water. Who by sword and who by animal.

Who by hunger and who by thirst. Who by earthquake and who by plague.

Who by strangling and who by stoning.

Who will have rest and who will wander.

Who will be at peace and who will be tormented.

Who will be at ease and who will be troubled.

Who will be rich and who will be poor.

Who will be brought low and who will be raised up.

But Penitence, Prayer and Charity avert the severe decree.

The Russians march across the border on September 17, 1939.
THE WAR STARTS.

The Polish, they don't fight too much by us.
3-4 days after, a **Nachalnik**, a party man,
and soldiers come to Germakivka.
The Communists take over.
They manage the police, the trains,
the post office, **everything**.

They call my family,
all the Jews, "rich capitalists."

The Nachalnik wants
now to investigate us.

But my father,
he knows
how to take
care of
the family.

My father has an idea!

Years ago, when he lived in America,
he brought home a lot of watches
to Germakivka.
I remember
a beautiful golden pocket watch with a chain,
and ladies' watches, platinum, gold.

Also... You know, he has a friend working
for the "People's" Governor of
our Oblast, district,
in the city of Tarnapol.

This friend helps
the Father
make up
a meeting
with
the Governor.

And you
know what?

While the Governor is sitting
by the desk,
my Father slips some of
the watches into the man's pocket.

They have a "deal."

Just like this we are no more
"rich capitalists."
Can you believe such a thing?

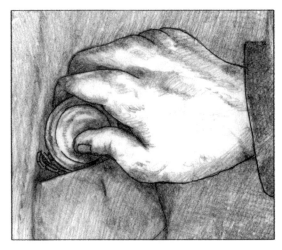

It's not so bad for us with the Communists.

Even **Yetala** and **Regincha** get a job in the Agriculture Department.

They do the office work.

But everybody don't have it so good.

I tell you the story of **Shunik**, a son of our next-door neighbor, **Guchinsky**. We always think this **Guchinsky** is a lucky man. He lives in such a beautiful house and he has two good boys. But you know, always, everything changes.

Yannick was the youngest son and they took him in the Polish army. When the German-Polish war started, he fell into the POWs and he disappeared.

Yannick

The oldest was this **Shunik**. He was a nice boy. Always happy. He likes a joke, fun.

Anyway, the **Nachalnik,** the party boss man, wants Guchinsky's house for himself, for any money. He wants to move in.

So what happens is he befriends this **Shunik**.

Yes, the **Nachalnik** befriended **Shunik,** but you see the **Nachalnik** was sneaky.

I'll never forget this story.
Everybody had to give to the Communists.
They taxed you,
so much chickens, so much eggs, so much milk.

One day the Nachalnik and other men
came to Guchinsky's house for the taxes.
This Shunik is sitting, and by him, he has
a beautiful cat.
"So I'll give the government the meat from
the cat for the taxes," he joked.
He knew all these guys.
He thinks he is with friends.
But, this same night they came
and they arrested him.

What a trouble it was for making a joke from the cat.

Sunday, the whole town has a meeting in the Polsky Dum, the Polish house.
It's like a social hall here. Everybody in town has to sign that they are called
to the meeting. So we all came in and they brought in this Shunik. The head
of the Communist party, this Nachalnik says, "Shunik told me that he will
raise his cat and when it will be big, he will give it for the tax. He wants to
feed our great undefeated Soviet army with a cat!"

So they gave this poor boy forever to Siberia.
And right away at night they send everyone
out from Guchinsky's house. In the morning
this Nachalnik moves into the house.
This I know
because
this I see
it.

62

You remember what happened to
your Aunt Yetala,
and the plate of potatoes?
I remind you.

First, you know, the Father and
the Mother love Yetala so much.
She was rough when she wants something.
They spoil her. If she wants something,
she don't ask, she demands. My
Father used to take her to Milnetze
or to Borchov to buy her shoes.
After the shoes he goes with her
to lunch.

Me, the Father, buys ice cream.

This is the youngest picture
I have from Yetala.

But, she is a special child.
Everyone in our town believes this.
I believe this, too.
How many babies are born
with six fingers on the hand?
Yetala is the only baby
I know from this. This is from God.

Later, the doctor cuts the extra finger off.

Yetala's story starts in the beginning from 1941.
Some *Roumainisher Menshen*, Romanian Jews,
escape to us, to the Russian part from Poland. Everyone was wanting
a *mitzvah*, and this was a big *mitzvah* to take care of these refugees.

You know we was having an
old lady,
maybe ninety years or more.
She was lousy and she was
kvechtzing, complaining.

I was washing her and combing her.
Her own daughter don't
do this what I was doing.

When comes **Friday night** we don't have fish for the Shabbos meal. Was the War.

I cook and **Jenny** cooks and
the **Mother** cooks. We cook
chicken. We cook potatoes.
We have a chicken soup and
a kugle. **Yetala** and **Regina**
don't know how to cook.
They are the younger girls.
They could play.
Yetala don't know nothing
how to cook when she grows up.
She don't have the responsibility.
Regina sets the table and
makes the guest welcome.
Yetala helps to serve the meal.

The Mother lights the candles and the Father says the Kiddush.
We have the Shabbos meal.

While we eat, this lady tells us what is happening to the Jews in her country.
"They are making pogroms," she says. "We are losing our businesses and houses.
They are beating us and killing us and hanging us up like pieces of meat.
This is not only the Germans who do this, but the Romanians, the Iron Guard."

Yetala brings out a plate of potatoes and asks our guest,
"Would you like some more?" The lady answers politely, "No... Thank you."

My Father has such a look on his face!
He tells Yetala he needs to talk with her in another room.

"How can you ask
a hungry woman
if she wants more potatoes?

Just you give her more
on the plate,"
my father says.

Oy, he is angry.

He is so angry, he gives her such a *patch*, a slap in the face.
He wants her to remember. He wants her to understand.

Mattaleh, you think this is too much? I don't agree with you.
I think, the father, he makes it right.

We hold this woman for one more month.
Then another family holds her for a month.

She passed away over there.

—June 22, 1941—

This day the Germans make war on the Russians.

The next day our life changes.... Again.

By us was very little shooting.

The Russians run away and the Hungarian Nazis ride into our town on the bikes.

They stay for three weeks.

And then the Germans come.

The Ukrainians are so happy. The Nazis promise them the freedom.

No more will **Germakivka** be for the **Poles** or for the **Communists** or for the **Jews**. Hitler promises the **Ukrainians** their own nation.

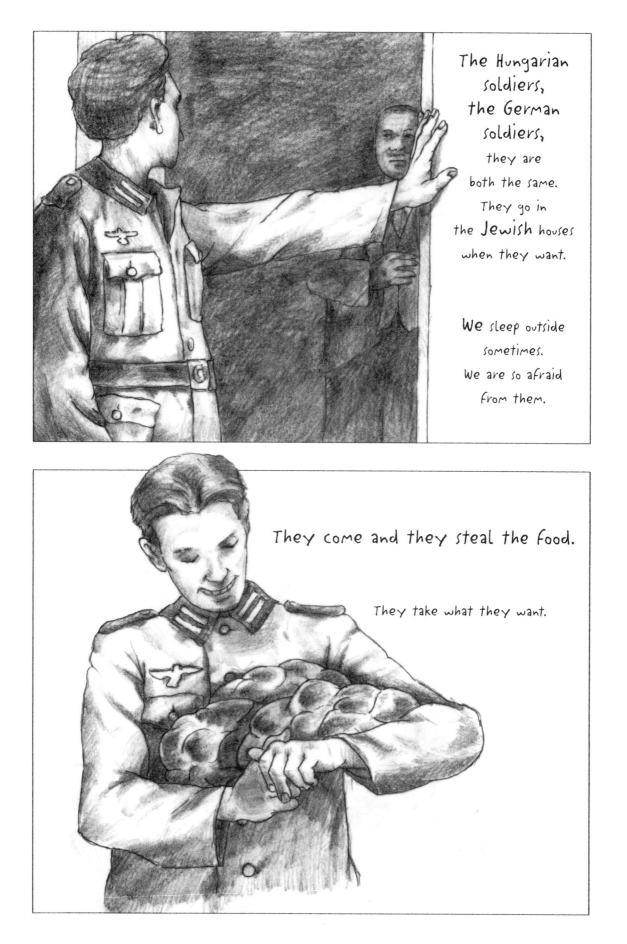

The Hungarian
soldiers,
the German
soldiers,
they are
both the same.
They go in
the Jewish houses
when they want.

We sleep outside
sometimes.
We are so afraid
from them.

They come and they steal the food.

They take what they want.

One time the wife of our next-door neighbor, **Mitri,** broke our window and she took a big stick with a nail and she was pulling things out from the house. We catch her, but what is the **father** to do?

Go to the police?

We, to that time, were well off. We had cows. We had horses. We had a wagon and we had a sled. We had a machine that cuts the straw. We had a lot of things not everybody in our town had.

So we started to give away our things to good Christian neighbors,
to hold for us.
We gave them away with the trust that we

will live over the war and we will get them back.

But, you know, these people were friendly before, but after...

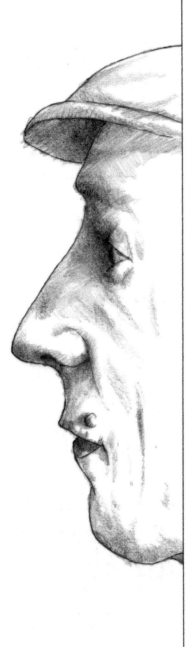

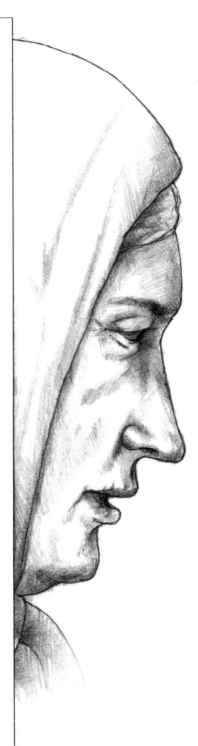

These Christians
became greedy.

They just wanted to keep
what we gave to them.

They never seen things
like we have.
What was it we give them?

Ha!

A pair of pants, a jacket,
a coat, a cushion, a top.
They didn't have nothing.

So, whatever they could
rob from the Jews
was good for them.

They think they will get
rid of the Jews
and they will be left over
with the things!

They will be rich!

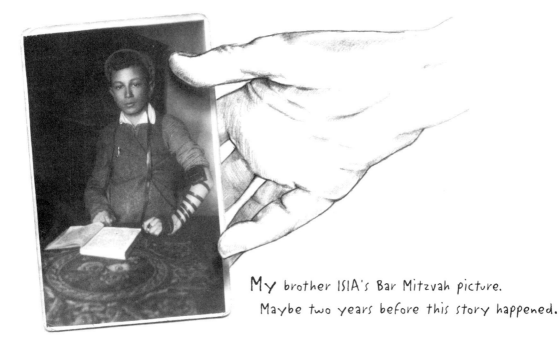

My brother ISIA's Bar Mitzvah picture.
Maybe two years before this story happened.

One time I was home and Yetala was home and Isia was home.
It was the time the Gestapo come into our house.

The Mother and the Father were out.
My FATHER went to the shoemaker and my MOTHER went to visit my married sister, JENNY.

This was such a cold day. It was in November, 1941. A NAZI comes and he wants a JEW should help push his stalled car. They was 3-4 soldiers there.

So the Gestapo man walked over to a **Sheygitz**, a young Gentile, and he ask him if he know where the **Jews** live. He wanted to call a **Jew** to push the car, and who knows what else.

So he came over to our house and he found me in the house. I go outside.

He wants my brother should help move his car. So I ask him maybe to let **Isia** to go in to take the jacket. It is so cold. I talk to him in **German**. I speak so good. I spoke so good with him that he understood everything.

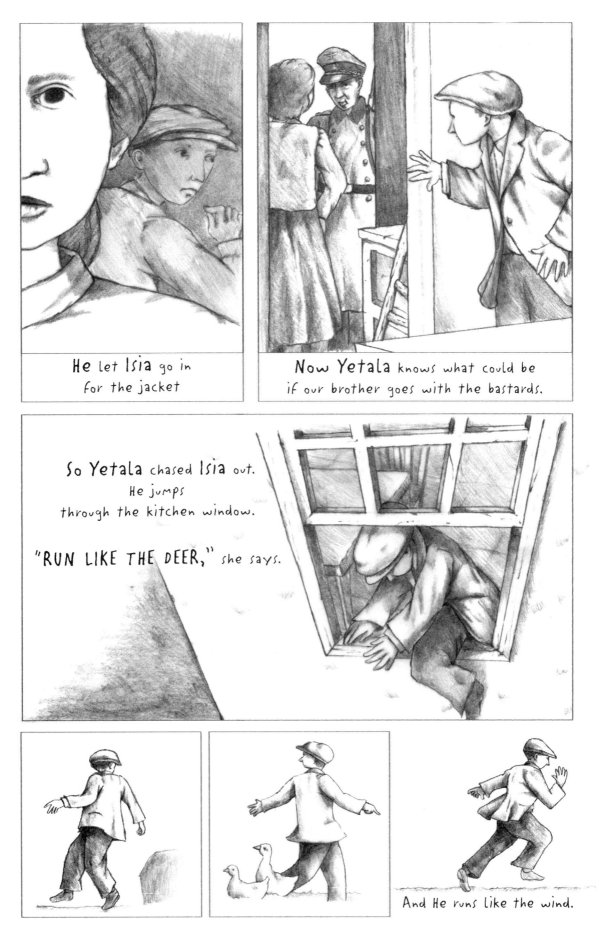

He let Isia go in
for the jacket

Now Yetala knows what could be
if our brother goes with the bastards.

So Yetala chased Isia out.
He jumps
through the kitchen window.

"RUN LIKE THE DEER," she says.

And He runs like the wind.

And then this **Nazi** realized that **ISIA** was not there.

"**Come inside with me**," he said. I said, "**No**," and I stood still like a **stone**. So still that if they  gave me a million dollars I couldn't move my legs. That's how stiff I was. He went into the house and he saw the windows were open... Meanwhile, I was standing, buried. I couldn't move. I couldn't move, because I was frightened. So then, when he came out again, he was very heated. Angry. **He saw that he lost his Jew. He** said to me again to come inside. If I would have come inside, he would have killed me.

On the street in that time, 1941, he still didn't have the right to kill us. So then he came over to me with the rifle. He turned the rifle over and he gave it to me on the head. In the street, there was peoples with cars, and with wagons. He hit me with the gun and, yes, the **Gentiles** with the wagons, with the cars, didn't do anything.

I believed I was going to be a cripple. He ran to me with such anger and he gave me such a hit in the head and by the ear that, pardon me, my period went. My period was pouring out blood and my ear was pouring out blood, and from my hair was pouring blood.

BUT I SURVIVED.
At night was everything in order. My FATHER comes home, my MOTHER comes home, ISIA comes home, YETALA comes home. MAYBE A MONTH LATER WE MOVED OUT.

They moved us out from there with all the JEWS in Germakivka. THE GERMANS want to concentrate the JEWS in the towns of Korolivka, Milnetze, Scala, Chortkov and Borchov.

We packed our clothing and our bedding.
Everything else we leave behind. We go.

The father drives to Korolivka,
to my Baba Bashi's house,
she is my Mother's Mother – Bashi Spitzer.

The Baba lived with my Aunt Zlateh and my Uncle Shmil Rosenblatt, her husband. They was so rich, maybe millionaires. He has the biggest leather goods store.

I don't think Rockefeller was so rich like my Aunt.

But you know even so, my Aunt feels my Mother is more lucky.

It's a sad story...

My Father has many children. His children live and grow healthy. But my Aunt Zlateh has children every year, but these children all die. So she says this to my Father, "When you have children, that's your luck. When you are rich is the wife's luck." This is a saying. She was only having two children that survived after the first day.

One was a very beautiful little boy.

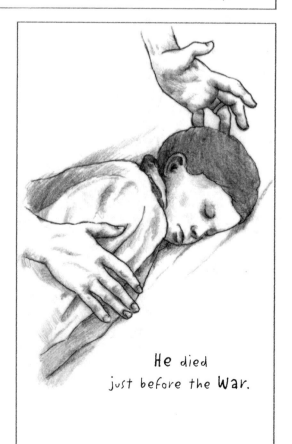

He died just before the War.

The other child my Aunt Zlateh has is a daughter about Yetala's age. We call her Chantze. In memory of Chunah's and Simon's Mother. Oy, you can't believe what a beautiful girl she is! She has blond hair like a Pole. You could think she was a *shiksa*, a Gentile.

I will tell you what happens to her later.

So for the next few weeks we all stay together in the Baba's house. We eat, we drink, we sleep, we live.

The boys, Simon and Isia, are not happy there. They want to go. They don't want to live in the Ghetto.

My Father don't want them to go. He is worried about his boys.

The Mother don't believe what she hears. "The world is upside down!" she cries. "I don't want to lose my children, too."

She don't want them to go, but, she don't know what to do. No one knows what to do.

"We will be all right," Isia says. "We can find a place to hide."

Simon, he tells her not to worry.

They will be safe. They promise her.

And so, like this, they went away.

Walking on the dirt street, they pass out of Korolivka. Across a small bridge, and up a big hill, they go.

This was the way to Germakivka.

But the Mother can't let them go just like this. She calls to them. She runs after them.

She has something for Isia.

Something to help them, and keep them safe.

"When I went on the hill, I don't know why, but I stopped," Isia told to me years later. "I see the Mother running. She ran after us. So we stopped. So she came over and brought me my Siddur, my prayerbook."

"That's my Bar Mitzvah Siddur.

I kept it through the War."

Through his whole life Isia keeps this, his Siddur, his Bar Mitzvah Siddur.

He keeps it to remember our Mother.

He keeps it to remind his own children.

Let my brother, Isia, tell you this part of our story.
He will tell you how it was with Simon and him.

"So Simon and I met up with the Director of the fields, near Germakivka. He was a good man, a Subotnik. He was from the the Christians who believe in the Shabbos. You call them Seventh Day Adventists. He was the watchman and Director of the fields for Grabuvosky. This Grabuvosky was a Graf, like a nobleman, very rich."

"Grabuvosky owned maybe 200 pair of horses. He owned maybe 1000 cows. He owned fields, woods. You know, the whole of the Maravinitz forest belonged to him! He owned, God knows, maybe a few thousand acres of land. The whole town worked for him."

87

"So when we came then to Germakivka from the Ghetto, we went to this Subotnik and he gave us a permission that we can work in the woods. We paid him with something. I don't remember what. The paper says that we are there to cut the wood.

So that's how we are able to go around free in the forest of Maravinitz. **Really this paper was unlegal.** It has no value. The **police** would not recognize it if they catch us. But, for us, it was good. The regular people believe this paper."

"**Yes,** this **Director** took a big interest in us."

"Now, next to his house lived a **Polack** by the name of **Bleider.** He was a poor farmer. He was a decent man. So the **Director** talked to **Bleider** and he told him that we will give this **Bleider** things if he will feed us and hide us in his house."

"I do remember what we give this **Bleider. My father** had a mink coat. The fur was on the inside. This we gave to him. And boots, all this stuff we gave to him."

"First Bleider thinks he can keep us in a hole in his kitchen, but very soon he realizes this is too dangerous. So, then, he has a better idea, to keep us in the barn with the animals."

"He dug
a hole in
the barn and
the cows stood
on top and
we were
under there."

"Every day it was easy for him to make
believe he brings water for the cows...

"but really he bring us the food."

"So, like this, our days go by."

"We hide in
the barn
or we go out
to cut the wood.

We learn
about the
**forest of
Maravinitz.**

Now we know
the woods good!"

Meanwhile, our life is hard in **Korolivka**.

The Ukrainians, the Silesians, the Germans, Everyone is a boss over the **Jews.**

We have to wear a white armband with a blue **Mogen Dovid on it.** It is maybe 10 centimeters big. The Nazis make us pay for this ourself. Oy, what trouble if we don't wear.

Every day it gets worse for us, but who could know what's going to happen? Was there any person that could believe in 1942 that Hitler will come up and make gas chambers and burn people?

My father thinks I am lucky. He used to say all the time to me "*Die vest leiben. You will live.*" He believes this, so he gives me goldwork, silver, you know, to bring or to give to this and this Christian. We hope they keep for us. I say to him, "Tateh, Father, why don't you carry it?" He used to tell me, "They kill Jews. I'm a Jew, and they will kill me." That's what he say and this I don't like.

I don't believe in this.

I say, "No, you kill first.
When they kill you,
you kill them first. If you get hit
you have to hit back. You can't let them.
He don't agree with this.
The Rabbis and the religious say
our trouble is from God.

The Germans are smart. They don't need to watch over us all the time. They have the *Judenreiter* for this.

A *Judenreiter* was the Yiddish police. They get the orders from the Germans to get them so much and so much peoples a day for the Lager, the work camp, or for worse. That was robbery. The *Judenreiter* should prevent. They should fight for the Jews. They should help the people. They help the Nazis because they say this is how they will survive.

This story happened in June 1942. This was before the Action.

One of these *Judenreiter* was very bad. This *Judenreiter* says to the Father that he needs to take me to the Lager, the work camp, to work. "The Germans need some Jews," he says. This bandit, this scoundrel knows MY Father will give him money.

My father paid. Yes.

But this is not enough for this *Judenreiter*.

-The Judenreiter makes a Deal-

He will take the money and the **mother** also has to go in my place.

The father knows that when she goes, she will come back. He knows I will never come back. They will rape me. They will take me and I will never see more the world. This deal happens and I was crying for **God** to help **my Mother.**

she goes and, thanks God, she comes back. The whole day she works by the fields until six o'clock at night. She works and then she comes back. Why didn't they keep her? Because that was how the order went. They took her only to work, like the **"fine people"** that they were.

Sometimes we believe we are going to survive
and sometimes we are believing we are going to die.

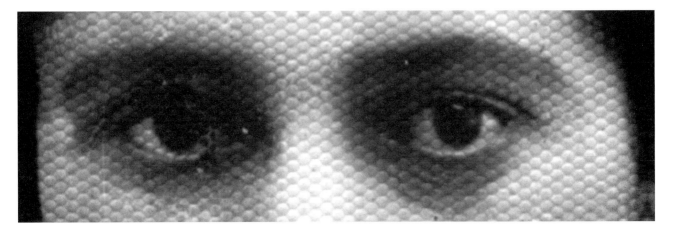

Ever since the German hit me, I was very afraid.
I was so afraid for a German, that I will die without a bullet.
But MY father says,
"They will take us to work, so we will go to work, nothing more."

Later there is no help for Yetala. There is no deal.
She goes to work in the Lager.

But MY father is a smart man.
He makes a plan for her to run away later.

-A week before Succos, the festival of Booths-

The first day of Succos fell out on a **Shabbos**, the 26th September 1942.
The Shabbos before, I have a feeling I need to go
to my brothers, **Simon** and **Isia**.
They was working in the forest near **Germakivka**.

We don't have the house in Germakivka no more.

I am feeling I need to leave **Korolivka**. Not for saving my life but
in my mind I am thinking I am going to the brothers so I can fix the pants.

When I come to the boys, what I take?
I take thread to sew up the pants.
The pants was tearing alot and they don't have a lot of clothing.
Do I care for me to get away, to live?
No... **Maybe no.**
I care for fixing the pants.
You know, they work. They have torn pants.

Maybe I **am** thinking
I go to save my life.

If not why am I wearing so much clothing?
I am putting on a regular dress and
also a flannel dress. Over these I
put on a sweater, a blouse, a skirt, a coat.

Yes, I am not coming back.

I put the thread in my bag.

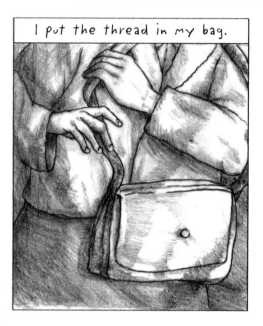

When I am ready to go
from the home, to go away,
my father comes over
and starts crying.
He is saying,
"They kill two girls
here, there,
by the **War**."

He don't want me to go.

I said to him,
"*Tateh*, *Father*,
when they kill me
you won't be to blame."
And I went out.
I don't say goodbye,
because he was crying.
I was crying,
that was this.

Oh, he loves, he
loves his children.

There was a boy going to *Kriftche*, he has over
there an Uncle. In *Kriftche* there was a
gerelna, like a factory, where they make
brumfin, whiskey. It was a very rich town
because of this. There was also
fields of sugar beet for
making the *brumfin*.
This helps us later.

Anyway, when he went, I say
to him, "If you are going
to *Kriftche*, I will go
with you. I am going to a
farm near *Germakivka*."

He takes me to the farm,
to *Simon* and to *Isia*.

Later this boy goes
back to *Korolivka*.

They kill him.

It is maybe 25 kilometer to go from *Korolivka* to *Germakivka*,
but with me, when we was walking,
we was walking around this way, around another way.
It feels like, maybe three times 25 kilometers.
We do this so no one should find us.

How do I find where my brothers hide?
My Father has friends.
Some good peoples know where they are hiding.

I come to the farm of
the *Subotnik*,
the Seventh Day Adventist
and his **wife**.
They are good peoples.
They are good Christians.

He can help me find the
brothers.

When I come to his house, is coming his wife to see me. To see who I am.

She takes me inside the barn where I will stay and she is helping me.

I take off the skirt, the blouse, the sweater, the flannel dress, and more. I have so much clothing on.

I took my comb, to comb my hair and, oy, you know what happens?

I took my comb to comb my hair and comes out maybe a million lice, a million.

I was sitting and crying and she come in and she saw me crying and looking at this lice, and she says, "You will have a trouble."

She wants me to move. To help me. But I couldn't move. Because we walk so much, the muscles strained themselves. On either side of my legs was like a bump, like an egg.

I want to go right away back to Korolivka.

I think, "What did I do? Why didn't I take the Father with me. Why I just cover myself? What did I do?"
I was not selfish. I think, "He would maybe go with me but I didn't ask him." I don't ask him. I don't say to him goodbye because he was crying, and I was crying.
I also ask myself, "Why I don't take the Sister's child, Eli? I could rescue him."
But after, until this day, I ask myself,
"Why I don't think about the Mother, too?"

104

Simon, a little after the war.

Isia, just before the war. The fence still survives in Germakivka.

Later, I wait outside for my brothers
to come back from the work in the forest.
How happy can I be to see the both of them?
You can't believe!
A stone is off my heart.

I hide.

I stay on top,
in the barn,
in the hay.

I don't go out
too much.

People are
looking for
the Jews.

If they catch
me,
"och and vey,"
"woe and pain,"
for me,
the brothers,
and for the
people
who help us.

In the morning I come out to cook.
Then is sure no one is there.
I cook for the brothers and
for **Bleider** and his family.
I make good verenikas.

And so like this I was living for
a week, until **Friday**.

Friday, I look through
the barn.
Was a road by the forest.

I see the Germans driving
on the road
to Milnetze.

This is the beginning of the Action.

Like every day, my brothers, Isia, Simon, get up
in the morning to go to the work.
They are hearing the trucks, too.

They know what is coming.

In a minute, they come back to the barn.

Isia says to me,
"Put on the sweater,
put on the dress,
take everything!"

And good-bye.

We go.

On this same Friday, Yetala is still in the lager, the work camp. Succos, the festival of Booths is the next day, Shabbos.

The father sends a boy, a neighbor, to rescue Yetala.
This boy goes, in the night about 12 o'clock, to bring Yetala home,
for yuntif, for the holiday. So he goes and he takes her out
and they run away. They go up to our home in Korolivka.

In the night, after they escape,
a Shturmer, a Nazi, puts gasoline to the buildings in the lager.
The whole lager was sleeping. Was not just boys and girls sleeping,
was married women, too. They burnt the whole lager, with the peoples
and if someone doesn't take Yetala, she would be burnt, too.
"I could see the buildings in the lager burning," Yetala told me later.

SHABBOS MORNING

We are sitting in the woods.
I hear crying. I hear shooting. I hear everything.
Because you are in the woods, you can hear a million miles.

Everything you can hear.
Everything, you think, is near you.
Now, this sound comes from the town of Milnetze and
all the shtetlach, all the villages, from all around.

So what happened?
The Subotnik come to us. He can come easily in the woods.
He says to us, "They are killing Jews."

The Jews, they gather them all together.
They take them to the Concentration Camp.
On my finger I have a zenichika, a blister, and this hurt me a lot.
Gottenu, my God, I can't tell you. This closed my ears,
so I shouldn't hear so much the hurt and the crying.

After the shooting, the trains come.
Through my forest, the trains traveled.
The people cried so, on the trains.
Did I see the trains? No, the trains I could hear, not see.
I hear the crying like was near me. So it pulled on me.
So it was.
We was not going back to hide in the barn.
Simon and Isia went one time more back, but not me.
They left me on this place I should sit, and they will come for me.
And they come back, and we were having an axe. The boys took away the axe.
What we forget in the barn, they also took away.
We cannot go back no more. And we was sitting in the woods.

We was sitting in the woods until the crying stopped.

It was until six o'clock.

So then we was sitting
and we hear
the trees shaking.

What happened?

A wild pig with baby pigs went by.
We was sitting about six feet away.
We looked at her and she looked at us.
The boys were working three or four months, so they smelled of the forest.
The pigs went by and *Chas ve shulam*, heaven forbid,
someone touches a baby, the mother would kill.

She left us alone.

I saw all this, and I hear all this,
and I was mute.

I said to myself,
"The WORLD is going under."

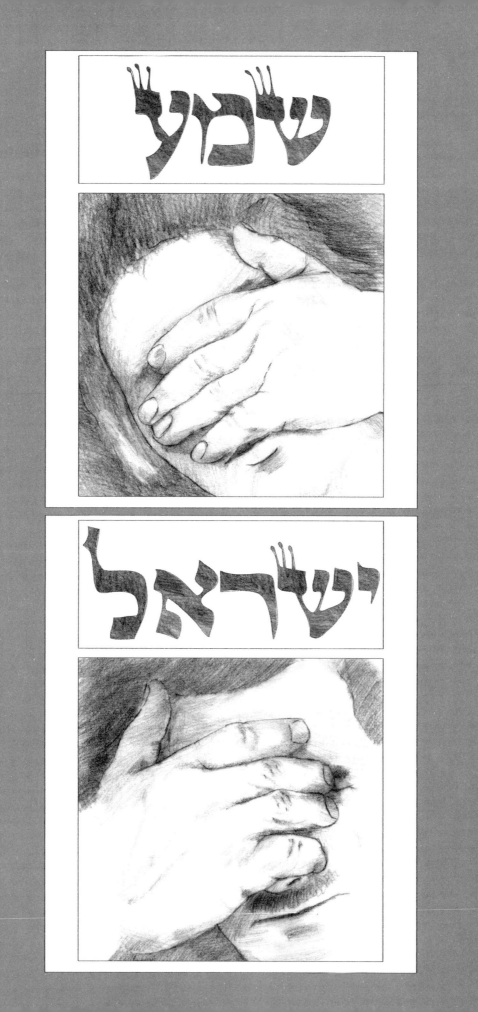

This is what happened that day.
What I tell you now,
Yetala told to me.

The morning comes,
The Action begins.
This is the end of the
Jews of Korolivka
and all the villages around.

"JUDEN RAUS!"

It don't matter if
you are a rich or a poor Jew,
a Rabbi or a thief.

It is enough for you
to be a Jew.
Your time is up.

"LOYF, YIDIN! RUN, JEWS!"

The Jews run. My father, Yetala, everyone.
The Nazis already encircled the *shtetl*, the village of Korolivka...

My Mother is betrayed by our neighbors from across the street.

These neighbors were caught first.

The Germans say to them, "Tell us where there are more Jews and we will let you go."

So they showed them where my Mother hides, and they find her.

They don't let the neighbors go.

The Mother doesn't want to go with them, so they beat her badly.
They beat her and then they took her.
They take my Mother away.

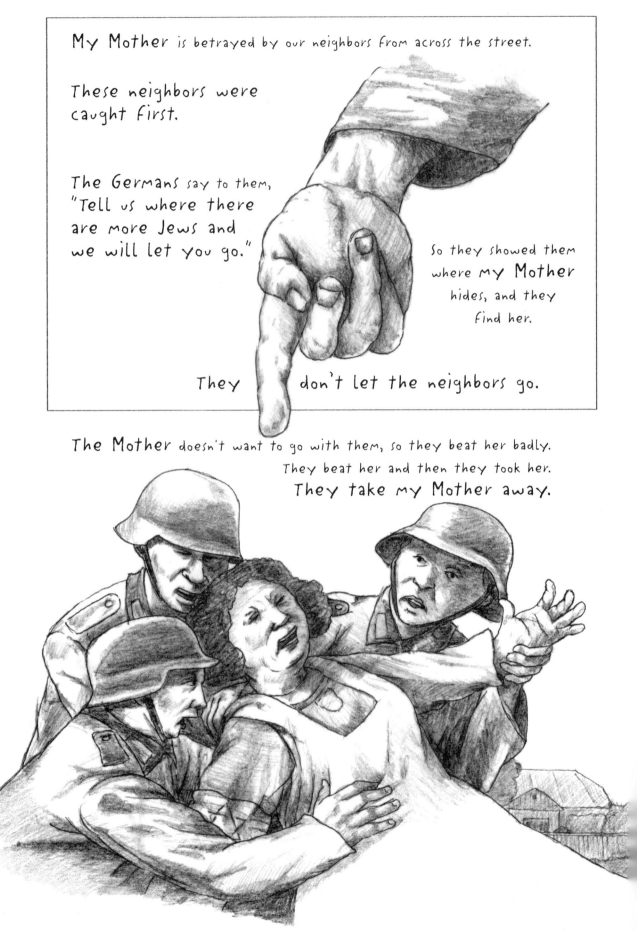

120

Yes, they took the Mameh.
Regina they also took,
and Jenny they took,
and her husband, Feivel,
and their child, Eli,
and the grandmother Baba Bashi.

I never see them again.

The Nazis, they caught the
Jewish people.

My father was running with the people, with Yetala.

The Ukrainians watch.

Such a good show!

She runs and she hears,

"Yetala, where are you going? Where are you running?"

"An Angel called to me," Yetala told to me.

The Nazi aims the gun.
He shoots and he shoots.

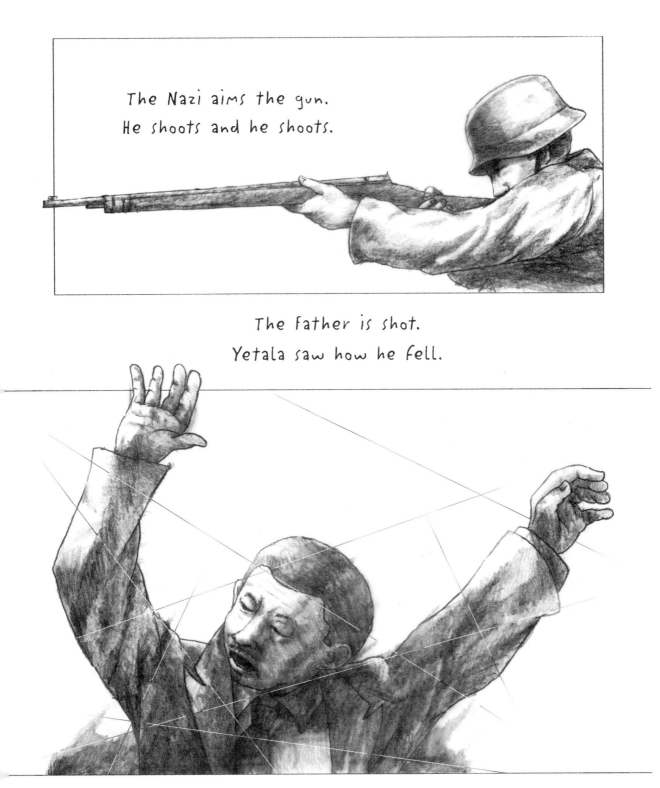

The father is shot.
Yetala saw how he fell.

He fell and she was left.
She strongly cried.

All this Yetala told me.

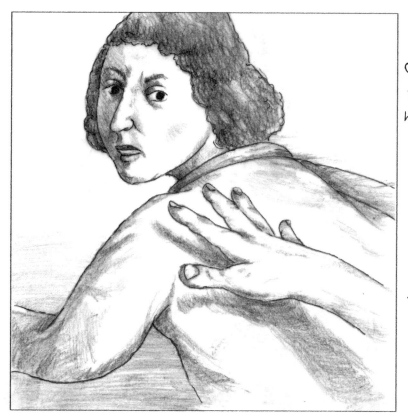

Quickly after this, the Angel touched her shoulder and said to her again, "Yetala, where are you going? Where are you running?"

She answered, "Oy, they shot the Father!"

So the Angel, he said to a Good Woman, "Take her, save her." The woman takes her and she is saved.

Did the Angel really touch her? I am not sure. I only know she was saved.

And so this Good Woman brings Yetala into the cellar
of the Uncle's house in Korolivka.
Inside this cellar was made a big hole, another room.
The Uncle built this room under where the koyman, chimney, is.

"Let her in," the woman says.
So Yetala goes in under the chimney with the other Jews.
In this room sits thirty peoples. The Aunt and The Uncle also.
The wall is closed up and then another man, not a Jew, hides it nice.
From outside he puts chairs, and all the furniture over the opening.
You would never believe that something is over there inside.

From inside they hear shouting,
"Juden raus! Juden raus!" "Jews out! Jews out!"
The Germans hit with their rifles to see if anyone was there and
then they went away.
Until six o' clock was the Action.

The Nazis catch most of the Jews. They put them in wagons and take them to Ivana Pusta. From Ivana Pusta, they go to the concentration camp.

And they took the Mameh, and they took Regina, and they took Jenny and they took her husband, Feivel, and they took their child, Eli, and they took the Baba.

They all died later... Nobody was left alive from them.

After six o'clock you could go out.
The Action was over.
"But, I waited until late at night to go out from the cellar,"
Yetala said.
"I wanted to find the father."

She walks back to where he was shot and finds where he lays.

You want to know something?
Over here lays the **Father**.

And over there lays the **Judenreiter**.
This bad man.
At least this makes me happy.

She sees our father is shot in his head.

—Later, the Subotnik told me he was alive the whole day.—

The father lays by the bridge for the whole day
and he begs for a little water.
To live, oy, to beg for a little water.

But nobody gives him.

Nobody gives him and this is, this is terrible.

The Poles, the Ukrainians, they say they was afraid.

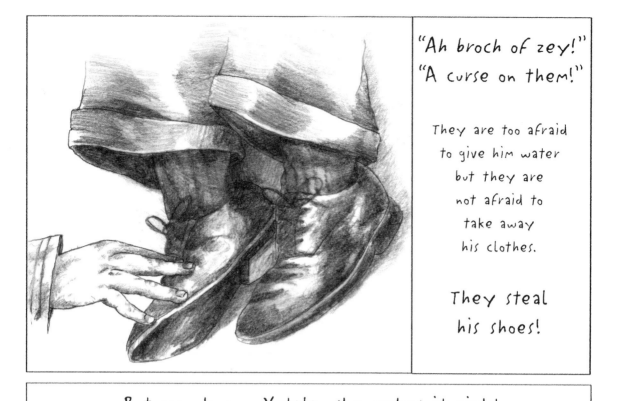

"Ah broch of zey!"
"A curse on them!"

They are too afraid
to give him water
but they are
not afraid to
take away
his clothes.

**They steal
his shoes!**

But you know, Yetala, she makes it right.

She hides him.
She buries him.

Yetela saw him
late at night
and the next
morning
she buried him
in the cemetery.

I was
on the grave
after the War.

129

And so that was the story of how they killed our family.

I didn't know
this story right away.

My brothers know,
but, they
don't tell me.

They see I am homesick.

They don't want me
to cry.

Isia would tell me of Milnetze, of Kriftche, from Borchov,
from Ujiran, from Scala, from Nivrev and from Zalicia.
He would tell me who fell, who they took away.
Oy, oy, it hurts to hear this! It hurts because you know this person, that person.

From Korolivka he tells me nothing.
All the time he is telling me, "In Korolivka wasn't an Action."

After Yetala buried
the father,
she comes back
to the cellar.

Our Uncle thinks no one
will find them there.

They are safe.

He is sure.

My Aunt, my Mother's sister, was a
good person. Every day she was worrying
about me, Simon and Isia.
Every day she was crying
when she had something to eat.
She would always wonder, "Who knows
if the children have something to eat?"
The children, that was us, in the forest.
She was missing us terribly.

We find ways to get food. Some people help us.
One man by the name of
Josip Jerema helped us.
He was a wealthy man who lived
10-12 houses from us in Germakivka.
He was decent.
Probably, if not for him
we would never have made it.

A week after the Action
we dig a grave to live in and to hide
in the forest of Maravinitz.

But, in this first grave we don't have any *seichel*, sense.

Why?
Because when we went to
the bathroom outside
the grave, we don't cover
with dirt, with leaves.

We don't think
this can give us away.

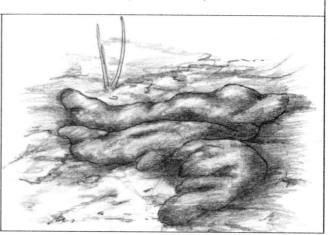

When you don't eat. When you don't have what to eat, you shouldn't know from this, we would make such a smell. And this is how they catch us.

Who catches us? No, not the Gestapo. The Goyim, the Gentiles, the Ukraina, they catch us. They look for us so they can kill us and steal what little we have. We are lucky. These Ukraina who catch us, don't kill us because they knew our Father. My Father was a good man and they like him. When they see this is Mendel's daughter, when they know that here was Mendel's children, they let us go.

We run 3 miles away from our first grave, and Isia and Simon make a new one for us.

Our new grave was ready on Friday, but we don't move in.

Why?
Because I said to my brothers,
"No! Not yet. Now we wait
until Tuesday to go in."
Tuesday was my lucky day.
My father said that.
I said, "**Tuesday** we go in, and in
a **Mazaldiker Shoo**, a lucky hour,
we will live."
We were bothered by the cold and rain.
But still, we wait until Tuesday.
We slept on the ground, wet and cold.

(You know **Tuesday** would taka,
really be our **lucky day**.)

So Yetala was hiding in the cellar, in the Uncle's house.

One night my **father** comes to her in a *chulim*, a dream. He says to her, "Don't be afraid. You will live. **Two Gentiles will come to you and you should go with them.** You should walk after them and you should not be afraid."

The next morning
she went to the Aunt,
and told her this dream.

The Aunt tells to her,
"*Mendele ruht nisht.*
Mendel doesn't rest."

This same day
Simon and Isia
find two womens to take
Yetala into the forest.

They pay these womens
with something.

On that Tuesday
the two womens go to
get our Yetala.

So she can be with us.

These womens know where **Yetala** is hiding. They know where we are hiding.

She walks behind them when they take her into the forest.

Tuesday we go into the grave.

Isia knows when **Yetala** will come to us. He keeps this secret from me.

In the time when she is coming, he goes out of the grave and says to me, "I'm going out to cook kasha." I say to him, "What?" I don't understand what my brother is talking about.

In that minute I hear **Yetala's voice.** I hear her speaking.

I go out and I look, and I see Yetala is here.

As I saw her, I finally understood that this was what is left from our family.

I sobbed so. Now the brothers finally let me cry.

And that's how it was
with me.

The whole night,
I heard Yetala talking.
Oy, how much I was crying.

Yetala told me about how
the Father was killed.

But, really,
as soon as I saw her,
I realized this was it.

I didn't believe my Father was dead until somebody told me.
A mensch is just a mensch, a person is just a person.
There isn't such a thing that if you are not totally sure that someone is dead,
to believe that he is dead. You can't admit it. You have to know for sure.

Yes, I finally knew...

The Father was dead.

The Mother was taken.

Jenny was taken.

Regina was taken.

This is what happened to my Aunt, my Uncle and their daughter.

My Aunt wants so much to save her only daughter, Chantze, so she sent her to a Christian family.

The girl went to church. She was blond. Her parents paid so she can be a person, a Christian.
But, you know, the daughter pined after her Mother.

For this reason the Germans find out she is Jewish. She don't have seichel, sense. She can't keep the secret. It's too hard for her. She misses her Mother.

This is also how they find out where her Mother and Father are hiding.

This man who was there told me this story.

He went out from the cellar and was in the outhouse. He saw what was happening already, so he didn't run back.

That's how he saved himself. And he told us what happened. How they kill thirty people.

So what does he hear? What does he see?

He hears how they go to the cellar and push away the furniture that hides the people.

This is, for the Jews, the end.
The Nazis pulled them from the cellar.

They took Chantze to her Mother, and on the way they shot her.

She was not dead yet, only wounded.

They brought the Mother
her wounded daughter for a present!

And then they killed the *present*, in front of the Mother and the Father.

After,
they shoot
the Mother
and
the Father.

We lived in the woods for two winters.

Every time we think we will be discovered, we moved away
and we digged another grave.
We would find a spot and make a hole maybe four feet deep
and maybe five, six feet long—like a big table.

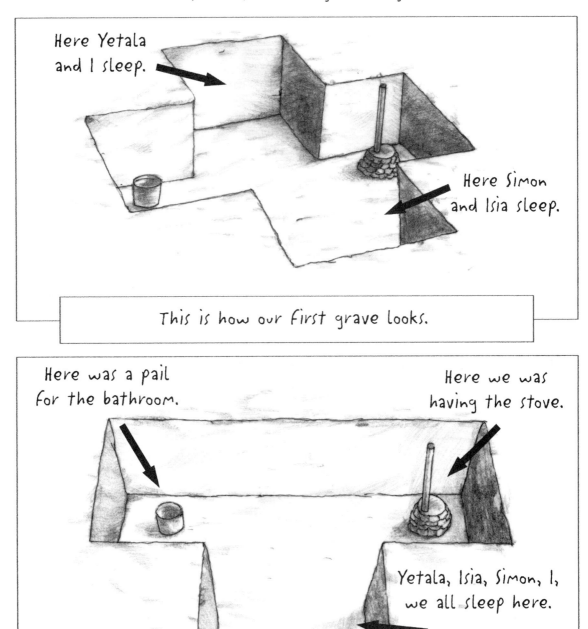

Here Yetala and I sleep.

Here Simon and Isia sleep.

This is how our first grave looks.

Here was a pail for the bathroom.

Here we was having the stove.

Yetala, Isia, Simon, I, we all sleep here.

This is how we make the other graves.
Simon and Isia was like engineers, making the holes.

We covered up the top from the grave with wood and with leaves.

Over here we was coming out. We was making here a door from some pieces of wood in a sack tied up.

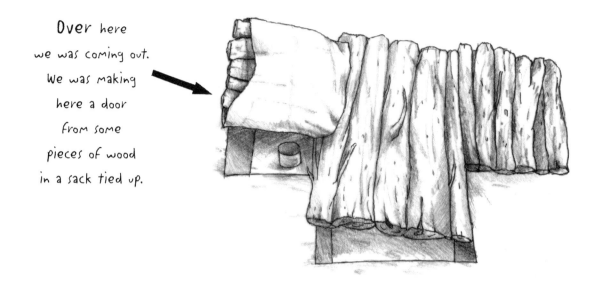

Sometimes, no matter how we covered up the door from the inside we couldn't cover it up right.

So the Subotnik came to the woods and covered us up nice with leaves, so our grave couldn't be recognized by nobody.

He also told us about the Jews they take away.

We make our stove out of stone.
On top we have a chimney.
But the chimney we put
down in the daytime.

At night is when I cook.

At night I was not afraid
because nobody
would come into the woods.
You could cook a potato
at night
because no one
would catch us.

In the day we was afraid
from the people because
they will kill us.

At night
is like the night scare,
a cemetery.
You wouldn't want to go
to a cemetery.
The Ukraina were afraid
from this,
from the ghosts.

Yes, at night Simon and Isia went out
to bring the wood and
to bring the water.

At night, I and Yetala cook the food.

I remember one time in the winter we make a big mistake. We build our grave maybe one hundred fifty feet from a main road. Very nearby, lived our Subotnik, the watchman for the woods. We hear a lot of talking, so we looked out and we seen the Ukrainian police in the black clothing. They came to the Subotnik's house and they have a whole party going on.
We was right there. We heard every word.

Isia, you know, was nervous about this. He wants to run away.
I say to him, "Where are we going to run to, Isia?
Should we run to the Father? Should we run to the Mother?"
We stayed and we survived... Later, we digged another hole.

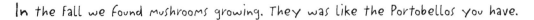
In the fall we found mushrooms growing. They was like the Portobellos you have.

When you would cut
one mushroom up
and throw the pieces
on the ground,
overnight grows ten.
This was some magic!

I think because we
was, pardon me,
dumping our shit,
this was fertilizing
the ground.

We take these mushrooms
to eat.
We was also giving
the mushrooms to
the people
who was helping us.
We was supplying
a lot of families.

These people didn't have what to eat either.

We like the mushrooms, but to live we need the potatoes and the sugar beets.

From these two we survived.

My brothers was going to the fields in the night and stealing these.

From where did they steal this food?
Simon and Isia steal them from the rich Graf, the nobleman, Grabuvosky.
This all was from his big estate.

This man, he has fields and fields with potatoes. Also with the white beets.

These sugar beets was used to make the whiskey.

In Kriftche was a granya, a factory, where they make alcohol from the beets.

We steal in the summer and the fall because we knew in winter we will not have any food.

We dig new graves for the food.
Every night the brothers put more potatoes
and more sugar beets in the holes, for us, for the winter.

For water for cooking and drinking we have to go very far.
We don't have pails, just two small *tepalach*, pots.

Until you come home is half a pot. Because you spill it.

Water was a million dollars.

Three years I don't know
what means a bath.

We was all filthy.
We don't have water,
what to clean ourselves with.

But, I am lucky.
The period, I don't have.
The period don't come.

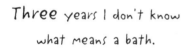

We use the pots for the water and also for cooking.

And so this was how we make the food. How we take the food.

Like this our days passed by.
The Winter comes.

And so we was ready.

"In winter the ground, it's warm. This was good," says Isia.

"I don't know where we have the strength.
There was times where we didn't go out for 3-4 days.

The girls didn't leave the underground."

"When the fresh snow came it covered up everything.
To go out we had problems
because we didn't want to show our steps."

We was worried they will find where we was hiding.

"Then we find a way of doing things," Simon said. "We found sticks that was 4 or 5 or 6 feet long.

We cut off the extra branches."

"Here we was stepping up on the branches," Isia told me.

"**We** trained ourselves how to hold ourself and we were walking with these sticks.
Where we walked it looked like an animal went through.
It looks like a fox track.
So we were walking and you could never recognize this was people.

You never see a human step."

This is how **the boys** bring the potatoes and no one catched them.

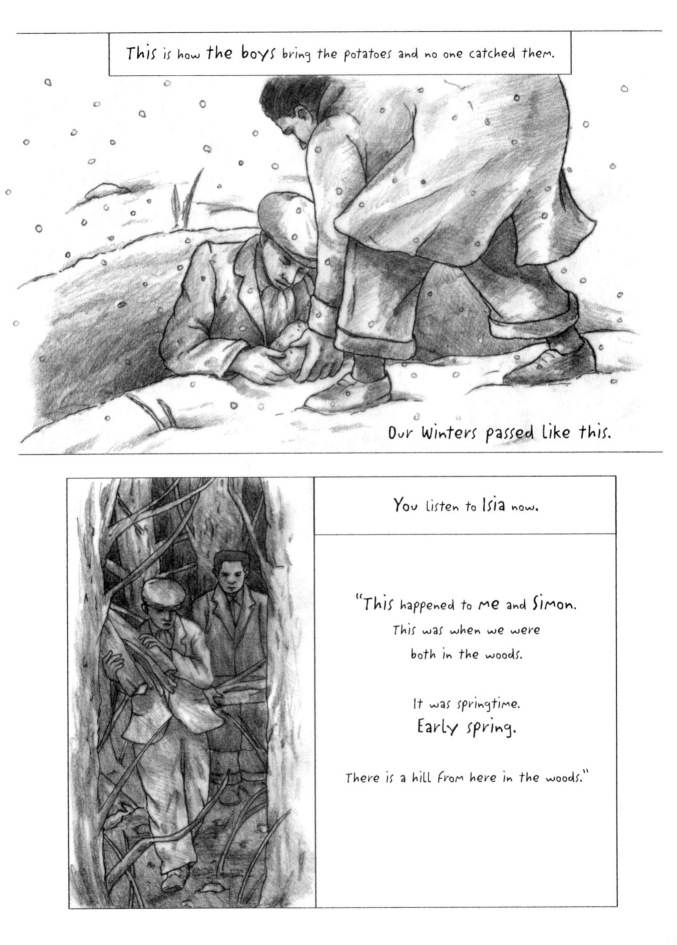

Our Winters passed like this.

You listen to Isia now.

"This happened to me and Simon.
This was when we were
both in the woods.

It was springtime.
Early spring.

There is a hill from here in the woods."

"And here was running water maybe two feet wide. It was just water that came down from the mountain.
It was springtime, so the water that was on top, was ice."

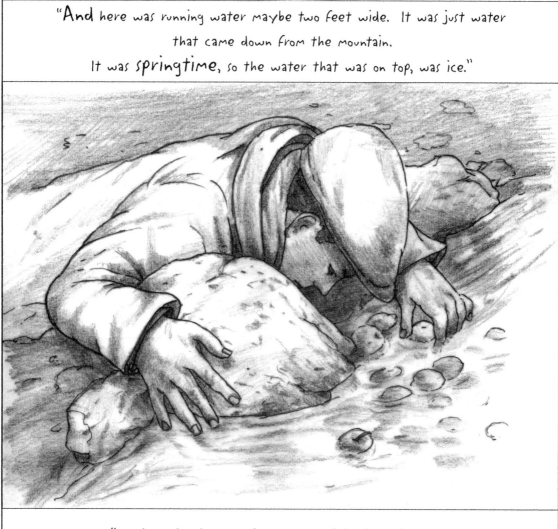

"But in springtime the ice started giving in a little bit.
All of a sudden there were crabapples."

"Some leaves or grass or something got stuck. So it couldn't flow.

The water was bringing down the apples.
They got stuck. They was floating up.

We find them apples."

"What a picnic!

I'll never forget.

We didn't get a stomachache.

Our stomachs,
at that time,
was so powerful."

You know, a few weeks later, Isia does becomes sick.
But not from the apples. From what, we don't know.

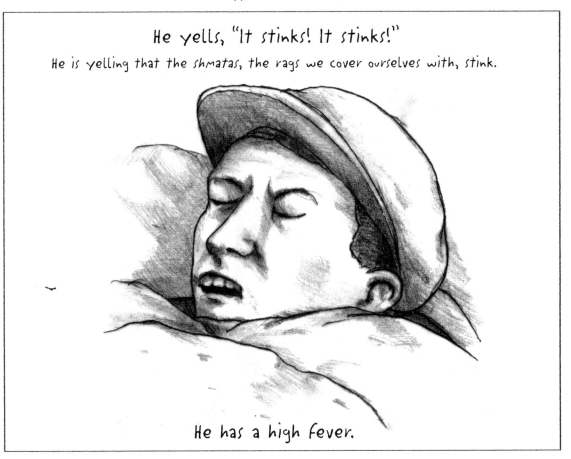

He yells, "It stinks! It stinks!"
He is yelling that the shmatas, the rags we cover ourselves with, stink.

He has a high fever.

So I go to a nun I know to get a sheet or a blanket.
Anything she would give me.

Maybe, a little wine, too.

I went and I asked for her, please, to give me help.

She gave me a half gallon of wine, not full, but some was inside. She also gave me some shmatas, and aspirin.

I came back, and then, Yetala and me, we wrap Isia up.

He takes the little wine and the aspirin.

After, I went away with Simon for water. We leave Isia with Yetala.

A little time later he says to Yetala, "I'm now healthy!"

That's how he answered her, "I'm now healthy!"
He became so warm.

In his stomach
the wine warmed him,
and pardon me,
he needed to urinate.

He got up, but,
he stumbled.

And he fell.

And as Yetala saw that he had fallen,

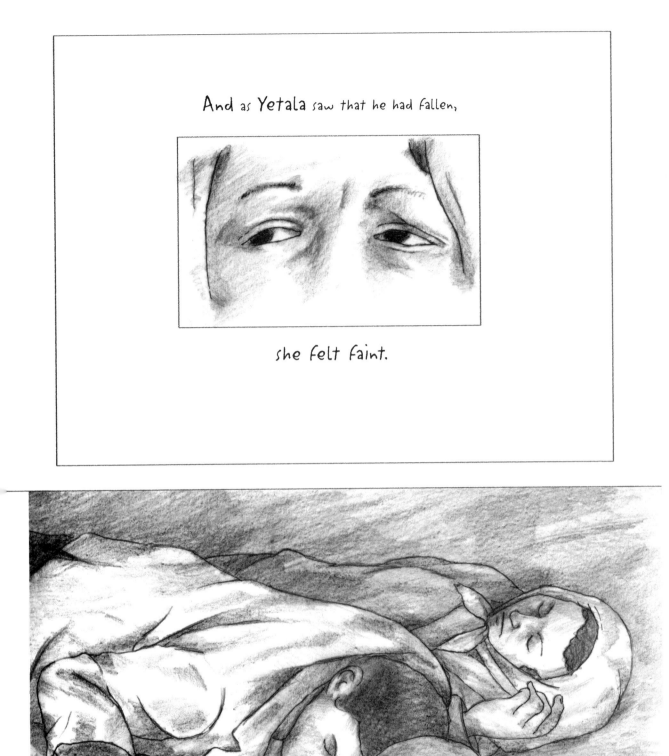

she felt faint.

And she fell, too.

When we got back
to the hole,
Simon sees them both
lying faint and nauseous.

So he took the water
that we was carrying for two hours,
and poured it on Isia and on Yetala.

Seeing them like this was just too much for me.
I couldn't take it no more!

When I saw all of this,
I felt so sick.

And I also fainted.

So what does Simon do? He throws the rest of the water on me!

That day we lost all the water.
Water, oh, water.

Who could believe that the German army coming back to Germakivka would be the beginning of our liberation?

This time, thanks God, they was coming from the East, running away from Russia.

173

When they reached
Germakivka
they kicked the peoples
from their houses.
The **Poles**, the **Ukrainians**,
they was all the same
to the **Germans**.
The soldiers needed places to sleep.

They was in **Germakivka** maybe two days.
Then, I think, they ran back to **Germany**.

A few days after, the Russians came.

We heard the head of these soldiers was a Jew.

I think maybe he was a General.

The second night after they came,
we went out from the forest,
into the light.

Soon after we was brought to this Russian officer.

When we met him we told him where we lived during the war and how we survived. He didn't believe us. He thought we was lying to him. He didn't trust us.

He thought maybe we was spies!

He wanted proofs.

So we told him, "Come into the forest. We will show you the graves for the sugar beets and the graves with the potatoes. We will show you the grave where we lived."

He came into the forest and we showed him our little holes in the ground. "Oh, I can't believe what I sees," he said. "I just can't believe how you live." This was from this officer who was in the army for many years.

So now we was free to go back to our house in Germakivka again.

But, you know, now lives a Christian family in our house.

They let us in

to our own house.

The lady is not very happy to see us.

I don't think she expects to see us again.

The peoples made themselves at home in our house.

181

What happened next was
Passover time 1944,
around the time we was free.

You remember, I tell you, we have
a beautiful garden with flowers.
We have lilacs,
like you have in your house,
Mattaleh.
By us comes up one white
one and two purple ones.

The nun, what gives me
the wine and aspirin
when Isia was sick, asks me to
give to her, to her church,
lilacs for Easter.
I'm so happy.
I give her so much.

The peoples living by us see
what I do
with the flowers.

The lady comes out of my house
and she yells,
"Why you pick so many lilacs?
Why you give so many away!"

I was so mad at her!
Here was this lady who yells at me.

She don't even own the house!

Ah, yes, but she <u>wants</u>
to own our house.

I didn't forget,
when we was hiding in the forest,
my brother Simon begged her
to give us bread, to feed us and
we would sign over the house.
This lady, her family, don't want to help us then.

Now when we came out free, she asked me,
"Is it true your brother wants to give us the house,
if we give you bread?"

"Why you don't give us bread when we need it.
What's the matter? You didn't have enough?"

For a short time more
we lived in our house
in Germakivka.
But, you know,
we was afraid to stay.

Even with the war
over for us,
Ukrainian bandits
was still killing Jews.

Oy, how they all hated us.

So, we eat for one last time in our house.
I take the Father's wine cup, I take some of the Mother's
needlework, and I take the photographs from our family.

And good-bye.

We go.

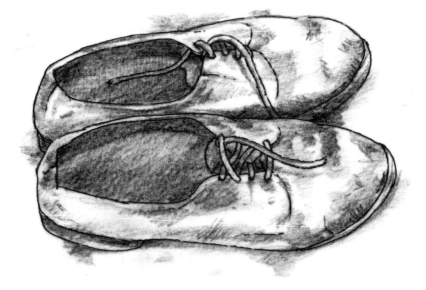

מוסף ליום כפור

בְּרֹאשׁ הַשָּׁנָה יִכָּתֵבוּן • וּבְיוֹם צוֹם כִּפּוּר יֵחָתֵמוּן •
כַּמָה יַעַבְרוּן • וְכַמָה יִבָּרֵאוּן • מִי יִחְיֶה • וּמִי יָמוּת • מִי
בְקִצּוֹ • וּמִי לֹא בְקִצּוֹ • מִי בַמַּיִם • וּמִי בָאֵשׁ • מִי בַחֶרֶב •
וּמִי בַחַיָּה • מִי בָרָעָב • וּמִי בַצָּמָא • מִי בָרַעַשׁ • וּמִי
בַמַּגֵּפָה • מִי בַחֲנִיקָה • מִי בַסְּקִילָה • מִי יָנוּחַ • וּמִי
יָנוּעַ • מִי יִשָּׁקֵט • וּמִי יִטָּרֵף • מִי יִשָּׁלֵו • וּמִי יִתְיַסָּר •
מִי יֵעָנִי • וּמִי יֵעָשֵׁר • מִי יִשָּׁפֵל • וּמִי יָרוּם •

בקול רם   צום   קול   ממון
וּתְשׁוּבָה • וּתְפִלָּה • וּצְדָקָה •

מַעֲבִירִין אֶת רוֹעַ הַגְּזֵרָה •

כִּי כְּשִׁמְךָ כֵּן תְּהִלָּתֶךָ קָשֶׁה לִכְעוֹס וְנוֹחַ לִרְצוֹת.כִּי לֹא תַחְפּוֹץ בְּמוֹת
הַמֵּת כִּי אִם בְּשׁוּבוֹ מִדַּרְכָּיו וְחָיָה.וְעַד יוֹם מוֹתוֹ תְּחַכֶּה לּוֹ אִם יָשׁוּב מִיָד
תְּקַבְּלוֹ • אֱמֶת כִּי אַתָּה הוּא יוֹצְרָם וְאַתָּה יוֹדֵעַ יִצְרָם כִּי הֵם בָּשָׂר וָדָם.אָדָם
יְסוֹדוֹ מֵעָפָר וְסוֹפוֹ לֶעָפָר בְּנַפְשׁוֹ יָבִיא לַחְמוֹ • מָשׁוּל כְּחֶרֶס הַנִּשְׁבָּר.כְּחָצִיר
יָבֵשׁ • וּכְצִיץ נוֹבֵל • וּכְצֵל עוֹבֵר • וּכְעָנָן כָּלָה • וּכְרוּחַ נוֹשָׁבֶת וּכְאָבָק פּוֹרֵחַ
וְכַחֲלוֹם יָעוּף :

מֶלֶךְ אֵל חַי וְקַיָּם :

...אֵין קֵץ לְאָרֶךְ יָמֶיךָ וְאֵין לְשַׁעֵר מַרְכְּבוֹת כְּבוֹדֶךָ
...שְׁמֶךָ • שִׁמְךָ נָאֶה לְךָ וְאַתָּה נָאֶה לִשְׁמֶךָ וּשְׁמֵנוּ קָרָאתָ
...לְמוֹ וְקַדֵּשׁ אֶת שִׁמְךָ עַל מַקְדִּישֵׁי שְׁמֶךָ.כְּבוֹד
...שִׂיחַ שַׂרְפֵי קֹדֶשׁ הַמַּקְדִּישִׁים שִׁמְךָ בַּקֹּדֶשׁ
(קוֹרְאִים וּמְשַׁלְּשִׁים בְּשִׁלּוּשׁ קְדוּשָׁה בַּקֹּדֶשׁ)
...נוּ מַלְאָכִים הֲמוֹנֵי מַעְלָה • עִם עַמְּךָ יִשְׂרָאֵל קְבוּצֵי
...לְךָ יְשַׁלֵּשׁוּ בְּדָבָר הָאָמוּר עַל יַד • נְבִיאֶךָ וְקָרָא זֶה אֶל
...דוֹשׁ יְיָ צְבָאוֹת מְלֹא כָל הָאָרֶץ כְּבוֹדוֹ : כְּבוֹדוֹ מָלֵא
...זֶה אֵיֵּה מְקוֹמוֹ סְכְבוֹדוֹ לְהַעֲרִיצוֹ לְעֻמָּתָם מְשַׁבְּחִים וְאוֹמְרִים

...אשִׁית.רַת וְכֶם הֵשִׁית.אָמְנָה יוֹם יוֹם
...בִּין : בָּאֲרָה לִשַׁעֲשׁוּעִים בָּהּ לִנְקֹת
...מְשׁוּעִים נִגְמַר בַּעֲצָתָהּ כֹּל בְּאוֹמֶר.נָשָׂה לַתְּכֵן

He spends his life earning bread. He is like a clay vessel, easily broken,
like withering grass, a fading flower, a fugitive cloud,
a fleeting breeze, scattering dust,

a vanishing dream.

EPILOGUE

So Mattaleh, you want to know where we go after we left Germakivka?
I tell you.
First, when we went from our house the boys and girls was separated.
I and Yetala went to Borchov.

Jews from Milnetze, Korolivka, Kriftche, Buchach, and Ivana Pusta came there to a displaced person camp.

Yetala   Me

They came from all over.

In Borchov we didn't stay long. There was nothing for us there.
To us, Poland was a graveyard.
We left for the Neu-Freiman camp in Germany,
with the hope we would be able to come to America.

Undzer choszewer mitarbeter Marjan Zyd (driter fun rechts) cu
it zajne frajnt, szef fun der landsberger D.P.-policej Berniker (
chts), undzer foto-korespondent G. Kadisz (cwejter fun rechts) un
ejter fun sanitets-amt in Landsberg h. Tabakin bajm farnichtetn
palac in Berchtesgaden. In dozikn palac hot Hitler ojfgenumen p
Chamberlain un premjer Daladier.

Yetala

Me

Damen oisznajder kurs in Neu-Freiman.

For Simon and Isia was different. They was taken into the Russian army.

The Russians take them away, to go to the front.

"First they trained Simon and me for two months in Sammarkand," Isia said.

"Yes, Simon and I saw each other, but we was in different groups. I was good in the army. I had a head on my shoulders."

"I was trained to point the machine gun."

Until this day, your Uncle Isia has two memories on his body from his time with the Russians.

"On January 25, 1945, I was wounded in the shoulder with a bullet. There is still metal in my body from it."

On his left arm he has a number tattoo, like from a person in a Concentration Camp.

How can this be, when we was never in the camps?

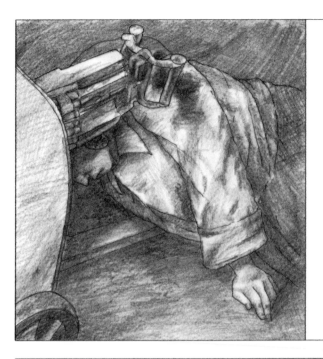

"Twice I was wounded.

The second time was
in the fight for Glywitz.

That day, there was
a lot of wounded soldiers.
All of us they put in wagons.
To go to the field hospital.

What happened next,
you wouldn't believe."

"Our driver became lost.

We was driving
around and around
for hours,
into the night.

Maybe he was drunk?

I don't know."

"Finally, in the dark we seen
a big cross, a red cross.
A hospital.

I don't know how he did it,
but this driver took us
to an English hospital.

A Russian hospital, he couldn't find."

"For three weeks we stayed in this English hospital."

"From there they sent me to a Russian field hospital in Opeln. And from Opeln they took me to a field hospital in Auschwitz. Yes, Auschwitz.

And finally I was in a regular hospital just outside of Lemberg."

"I spent maybe 3 months healing. Soon, I knew, they was sending me back to fight. But, for me, I had enough war. How much can one person take?"

"This guy from the Bricha, the Escape (a Jewish organization) has an idea how I can get away from the Russians. He's going to mix me in a group of Jewish Greek concentration camp survivors going back to Greece or Palestine.

You ask how can I become a concentration camp survivor?

Of course, I need a number tattoo on my arm. And this is what he gives me."

"Like so, I became a Greek Jew."

The day came and Isia went with them on a train to Czechoslovakia.

"When we arrived there the Greeks went on to their country and the Bricha put me on a transport of 30 trucks to the city of Gratz in Austria."

"From there I traveled to the Bari displaced person camp in Italy.

How was I spending my time in this camp? Mostly, I waited to go to America.

I was registered, but, they wasn't letting me into America so soon."

"You know, America don't let me in, but, Uruguay don't mind having a few more Jews.

And so I went to live in Uruguay. There I lived for 2 years.

In March 1950, I finally arrived in America."

For Simon, it was a little bit different story. He never went to fight with the Russians. When Simon finished his training, they put him on a transport to the front.

"From Sammarkand to the front is a long way," Simon said. "So we don't go straight. We halt to get water, to get food, like this. After many hours of riding we stopped in Lemberg."

You know your Uncle Simon. He was a friendly guy. He likes to talk, to make friends. **This was his character.**

"When we got off the train I started talking to some of the Jews that survived. They told me their story. I told them my story."

"They found a way to get me away from the transport and the soldiers."
And just like this Simon mixes in with the survivors of Lemberg.

"I changed my name and taking some few clothes, I wandered back
to around Germakivka,
to the town of Buchach."
In Buchach he stayed for a little time.
To put bread on the table, he is a manager of a small restaurant.
But soon this is not for him. He wants to find his family.

What is left of his family.

Soon again he picks up his few clothes and leaves to find us.
You know, Mattaleh, in that time all the Jews was looking for those who survived.
You hear all over, "Did you see this one? Did you see that one?"

"I found my sisters, in this way. I asked here. I ask there."

And he traveled to Neu-Freiman.

And after a little time Simon found us.

What is a DP camp? What is Neu-Freiman? I tell you.
(Before General Eisenhower visited us, it was like a prison.
After was much better. This is what was before.)

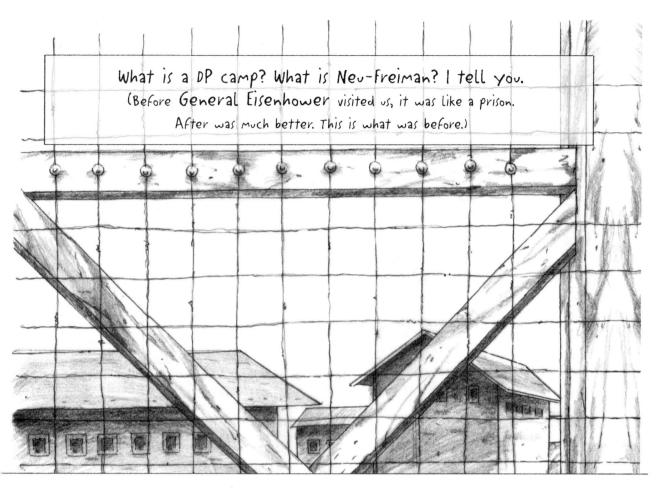

Neu- Freiman means new free man in German.
This is funny. The Nazis try to kill us all
and then after, the Americans put us in a jail.
We have food, but, we also have the gates and the wire and the guards.

Sometimes I don't understand
the guards, the soldiers.

One time I get a bag potato chips from them.

I don't know what's potato chips.
Can you eat raw? Do you have to cook?
I don't know. I never seen before.

So what do I do? I make a potato chip soup.
I cook with onion and a carrot.

It was good.

I meet your father in the camp.
He was a handsome man,
but also wild.

He wanted to be a *grosse macher*, a big shot.
One time he thinks the soldiers
will catch him smuggling.
I think he was carrying cigarettes or *bromfin*, whiskey.
So what does the *meshuggener*, the crazy one, do?
He pulls his pants down and acts like a mad man.
The soldiers don't know what to do.
They let him go.

כתובה

Soon after,
I marry your Father.

You know, Mattaleh,
I don't have such
a happy life
with him.

209

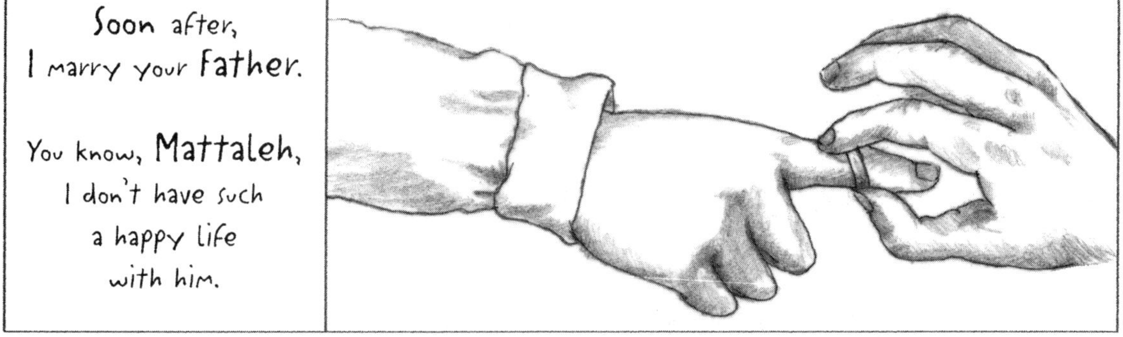

Everyone was marrying in the **Neu-Freiman** camp.
We all wanted to start a new life.

"In 1947,
I marry, too,"
Yetala said.
"But, you know,
I make a mistake.
My husband is
not a good man.
He hits me."

"I didn't survive in the forest
to live my life with a man like this!
In 1952 I divorced him.
It wasn't until
I came to **America**
that I met your **Uncle Kalman**."

"**Kalman** was a quiet man, a tailor, a gentleman.
We didn't have kids,
but still I lived a good life with him.
He was a little like a baby.
He was so scared that something
will happen to me. When I got lung cancer,
I was more worried for him than for me.
He was so scared to lose me.

When I died on November 8, 1987,
I think he went a little crazy."

Like Isia, your *Tateh* and I was registered to come to America.
But we have more luck. We don't have to wait so much.
But we have a problem, like all the survivors. We don't have no papers, no passport.
Instead, they give us this paper.

CERTICATE OF IDENTITY IN LIEU OF PASSPORT

AMERICAN CONSULATE GENERAL, MUNICH GERMANY

16719

Date   March 28, 1947

1. This is to certify that   Tovia LEMELMAN   , born at
(name in full)

Russia   Charkow   15th
(country)   (town)   (district)   on   (day)

of   January   ,   1909   ,   male   ,   married
(month)   (year)   (sex)   (marital status)

Gusta SCHAECHTER   , intends to immigrate to
(given and maiden name of wife)

United States

2. He (she) will be accompanied by   wife- Gusta LEMELMAN, born August 12, 1922, in
(Here list all family members by name,
birthplace and date, together with citizen-
ship of each)
Germakuwka, Russia.

3. His (her) occupation is   locksmith

4. DESCRIPTION

Height   5   ft.   3   in.

Hair black   Eyes olive

Distinguishing marks or features:

birthmark right corner

of mouth.

5. He (she) solemnly declares that he has never committed nor has be been convicted of any crime except as follows
none

6. He is unable to produce birth certificate, marriage license, divorce papers and/or police record for the following
reason(s) Above document has been destroyed and it is impossible to obtain
duplicates due to existing conditions following the war.
I hereby certify that the above are true facts, proper photograph and description of Myself.

Subscribed and sworn to before me this 28th day of March
1947.

Tovia LEMELMAN
Toiafu Lemelman
(Signature of applicant)

(signature of
(Date)

434-7-48

This is the *Tateh*'s. I lose mine.

211

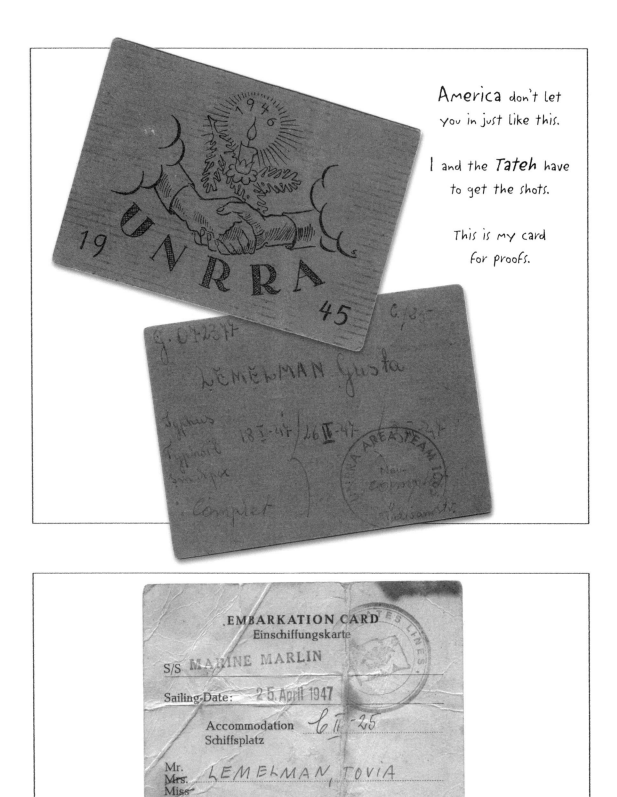

America don't let you in just like this.

I and the *Tateh* have to get the shots.

This is my card for proofs.

The Joint (the American Jewish Joint Distribution Committee)
helped us come to America.
A ticket from Bremen to New York was $200.00 with $8.00 head tax.

For me the trip wasn't so good. The boat shakes. I am throwing up the whole time.

Oy, but to see America. This was wonderful.

In winter 1946 we was still in the camp.
In spring 1947 we was on the boat.
And on the 6th December 1947,
I give birth to your brother, Bernard.

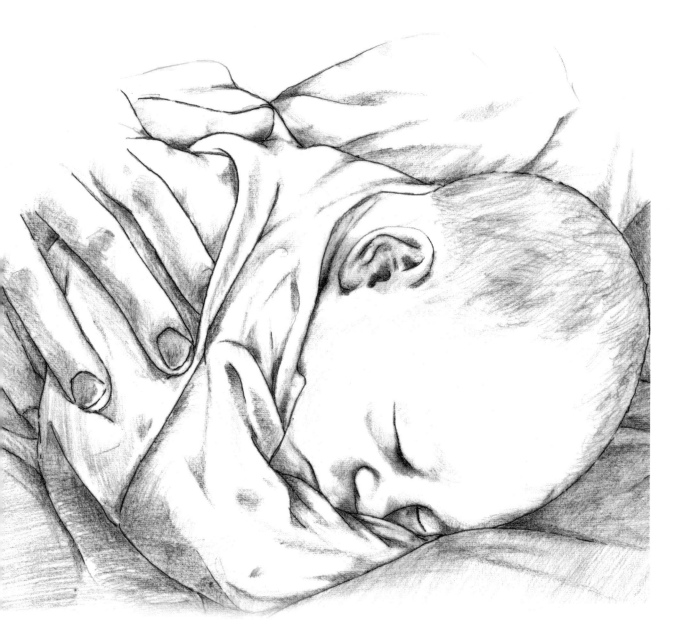

For me ... was a new life in America.

"Yes, this happened to me.

I ran and they shot me.
I was bleeding until I died.
My precious daughter, Yetala,
buried me."

The Father

"Yes, this happened to me.

I hid, but they found me, and beat me.
They took me to Belzec,
then Maidanek.
They gassed us, and burnt us."

The Mother

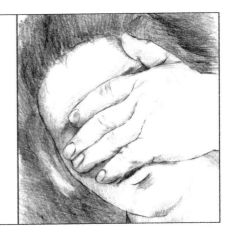

"Yes, this happened to me.

They took me,
and my husband, Feivel,
and my son, Eli.
They gassed us, and burnt us."

Jenny

"Yes, this happened to me.

I was taken with the Mother.
They gassed us,
and burnt us."

Regina

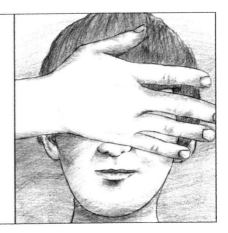

"In every generation, one must look upon himself, as if he personally came out of Egypt."
The Passover Hagaddah

Acknowledgments

You might say this book came about as a result of a frozen chicken.

Ever since I was a child, I was aware that my parents had survived the Holocaust. Other kids I knew had grandparents. Where were mine?

While growing up I heard a few stories about my mother's survival, but for the most part that experience was too painful for her to discuss with her kids in any real depth. And, she was also too busy working with my father in our candy store. She was always busy.

In 1989 (five years after my father died) she called.

"Mattaleh," she said, "I hurt myself and I can't walk so good."

"What happened, Ma?" I asked.

"Can you believe?" she said, "I drop a frozen chicken right on my foot. But, you don't worry. I be OK."

Of course I was worried, and of course I wanted to make sure she was OK. My wife, Monica, chased me out the door. "You have to pick up your mother today!" she said. So I drove to her house in Far Rockaway, and brought her back to Pennsylvania.

X-rays revealed that she did have a broken foot and she was ordered by my doctor to "take it easy" for six weeks.

My mother, however, never liked to take it easy. My wife and I were constantly badgering her to sit down. "No, you don't have to cook for us, Ma. No, please DON'T wash the floors." This went on for a week until I got the bright idea to ask her about her life, about her story. Maybe this would slow her down and make her sit for a bit. At first she was reluctant to talk.

"Feh, why you need to know all this," she asked. But she warmed to the idea and her experiences poured forth. Thank goodness I had the video recorder rolling.

What she told me is the basis of Mendel's Daughter.

I want to thank my **Uncle Isia, Isak Schachter.** He helped fill in parts of the story that were missing from my mother's narrative. He is a great storyteller and I really enjoy hearing him speak about our family.

Rob McQuilkin is a super agent and a wonderful person. I am grateful for his belief in my book. I knew he could "make it happen." I also want to thank his partner **Maria Massie** at **Lippincott Massie McQuilkin** for working so hard to bring this book to the rest of the world.

I'm really lucky to be working with **Martha Levin,** my editor and publisher at **Free Press.** Her enthusiasm is contagious and her support invaluable. I enjoy our "brainstorming" sessions on-line. I also value the help and hard work that my editor **Maris Kreizman** has put into making this book what it is.

I can't forget my brother, **Bernard.** He was the first person to believe in my work. I would never have chosen the path I did without his help. He actually liked my art—even when I was thirteen.

Thanks also to my sister-in-law, **Diane,** for telling me, after reading about eighty pages, "You know, this should really be published."

I want to thank **Jonathan, David, Benjamin** and **Sam,** my wonderful children, for being just that—**wonderful children.** They help me realize there are more things in life than work.

Finally, I want to thank my wife, **Monica,** for her honesty, perception and beautiful smile. I love you.

· About The Author ·

Martin Lemelman grew up in the back of a candy store in Brooklyn, New York. He is the child of Holocaust survivors.

His parents nearly *plotzed* when, at the age of 13,
he decided to become an *artist*. He has been a freelance illustrator since 1976, and has created art for over 30 children's books. His work has also appeared in numerous magazines.

Mendel's Daughter is a labor of love and obsession.
"He can't stop talking about it," his wife says.

This is his first book published by Free Press.

Martin is a Professor in the Communication Design Department at Kutztown University. He lives in Allentown, Pennsylvania, with his sweet wife, Monica.
They are the proud parents of four wonderful sons.